Managing Special Education

Codes, Charters and Competition

John Fish and
Jennifer Evans

OPEN UNIVERSITY PRESS
Buckingham · Philadelphia

Open University Press
Celtic Court
22 Ballmoor
Buckingham
MK18 1XW

and 1900 Frost Road, Suite 101
Bristol, PA 19007, USA

First published 1995

A catalogue record of this book is available from the British Library

ISBN 0 335 19438 9 (pb) 0 335 19439 7 (hb)

Library of Congress Cataloging-in-Publication Data

Fish, John.
Managing special education : codes, charters, and competition / by John Fish and Jennifer Evans.
p. cm.
Includes bibliographical references and index.
ISBN 0–335–19439–7, — ISBN 0–335–19438–9 (pbk.)
1. Special education—Great Britain. 2. Special education—Great Britain—Administration. 3. Special education—Great Britain—Finance. I. Evans, Jennifer Mary.
LB3986,G7F57 1995
371.9'0942'0941—dc20

95–8621
CIP

Typeset by Graphicraft Typesetters Ltd, Hong Kong
Printed in Great Britain by Biddles Ltd, Guildford and Kings Lynn

CONTENTS

Abbreviations

AWPU	Age Weighted Pupil Unit
CDC	Council for Disabled Children
CERI	Centre for Educational Research and Innovation
CFF	Common Funding Formula (for schools)
DES	Department of Education and Science
DFE	Department for Education
EA 1993	Education Act 1993
ERA 1988	Education Reform Act 1988
ESRC	Education and Science Research Council
FAS	Funding Agency for Schools
FEFC	Further Education Funding Council
FESC	Further Education Staff College
FEU	Further Education Unit
FHEA 1992	Further and Higher Education Act 1992
GCSE	General Certificate of Secondary Education
GM/S	Grant-maintained/School
HOC 1993 or House of Commons 1993	The Third Report of the House of Commons Education Committee 1993
HMI	Her Majesty's Inspector (of Schools)
IEP	Individual Education Plan

ILEA	Inner London Education Authority
LEA	Local Education Authority
LMS	Local Management of Schools
LMSS	Local Management of Special Schools
NFER	National Foundation for Educational Research
NHS	National Health Service
NTA	Non-teaching Assistant
NUT	National Union of Teachers
OECD	Organization for Economic Cooperation and Development
Ofsted	Office for Standards in Education
SAT	Standard Assessment Task
SEC	Special Education Consortium
SEN	Special Educational Needs
TEC	Training and Enterprise Council
ULIE	University of London Institute of Education
USA	United States of America

1 / Education and Individual Differences

A new beginning

A completely new framework for administering, funding and monitoring primary, secondary, further and adult education has evolved since the late 1980s. The process of change started by the Education Reform Act 1988 (ERA 1988) (DES 1988b) has been completed by the Further and Higher Education Act 1992 (FHEA 1992) (DFE 1992b) and the Education Act 1993 (EA 1993) (DFE 1993). A major outcome of the legislation is that individual schools and colleges are now almost entirely responsible for the quality of education delivered to the pupils and students they admit.

It will take some time before all the implications of legislation are recognized and implementation is complete. A local government review has recommended the creation of some new unitary authorities, while existing local education authorities (LEAs) are putting into effect new procedures. Implementation of the education legislation in some areas may well be delayed and interrupted by changes in local government.

Schools are now expected to deliver a National Curriculum and meet the varying educational needs of all their pupils. LEAs and the Funding Agency for Schools (FAS) are to be primarily concerned with ensuring that sufficient school places are available. They have very limited powers to plan and manage educational provision in an area. A Further Education Funding Council (FEFC) is responsible for financing and monitoring the effectiveness of independent post-16 colleges responsible for delivering a nationally agreed range of academic and vocational qualifications.

An educational market has been created based on parental preference, pupil and student choice, and funding policies. These, together with relatively infrequent inspections, are seen as sufficient means of ensuring equity.

All these changes have implications for special education. Primary and secondary schools now have clearly defined responsibilities to meet the special educational needs of all pupils who are not the subject of statements. LEAs remain responsible for assessing pupils who may require statements and for securing provision for those for whom they maintain statements. Parents are given greater choice and an independent Tribunal will hear their appeals against LEA proposals. *A Code of Practice for the Identification and Assessment of Special Educational Needs* (DFE 1994g) sets out procedures for schools and LEAs. The FHEA 1992 defines the similar responsibilities of the FEFC and of colleges of further education for students with disabilities and learning difficulties.

The nature of the educational market, with particular reference to special education, will be discussed elsewhere. However, minority and special needs are expensive in true markets and can often only be met with above average resources. Minority and special needs in an educational market often arise where children and families require social support as well as additional educational resources. As an Audit Commission/HMI report, *Getting in on the Act* (Audit Commission 1992a), states, the current system provides no inducements for schools to meet such needs.

The harder to teach

The provision of special education is only a part of a wider question about how society and schools respond to individual differences, some of which are seen as more acceptable than others. School policies have both explicit and implicit social values. For example, giftedness is more acceptable than limited ability, and good behaviour than disruptiveness. The approaches of schools to those who appear to be hard to educate or who have special needs of all kinds are influenced by parental, social and political views. A number of commentators have described and commented on the effects of these value systems (Ford *et al.* 1982; Tomlinson 1982; Barton and Tomlinson 1984).

The education system has always had difficulty in dealing with marked individual variations, particularly where pupils demonstrate very different learning styles, needs and motivation. 'Harder to teach' or less successful learners may be allocated less experienced teachers and more limited resources. They may be less attractive to schools and colleges which now determine their own admission policies. There is already some evidence of an increase in exclusions, particularly from grant-maintained (GM) schools (Cohen *et al.* 1994). It is far from clear, in some instances, whether it is parental or school choice which is being exercised. There is a danger that poorly motivated and reluctant pupils and students will have a limited choice of school or college, although the EA 1993 gives LEAs the powers to require schools to admit individual pupils.

It remains to be seen whether the new framework for education provides better or worse opportunities for the harder to teach. Current policies to improve national standards recognize successful 'academic' achievements but view meeting personal and social educational needs as of less importance (Wedell 1990). The changed educational system, of individually competing schools and colleges, raises the issue of how a market will meet social responsibilities for the education of harder to teach and unresponsive groups of pupils and students. It is necessary to ask:

- What are the social responsibilities of schools and colleges?
- How does the educational market deal with individual social and cultural differences?
- What is the range of individual differences for which schools and colleges might be expected to make provision?

Individual or institutional deficits?

Before the recent changes, it could be argued that maintained schools and colleges shared responsibility for pupils and students with their LEAs. It was possible to negotiate extra help for those with learning and behaviour difficulties and to arrange transfers to other LEA schools and colleges. Now governors and staff are totally responsible for the education of a pupil admitted to a school or a student accepted by a college.

The 'harder to teach' issue is particularly significant for special education. In addition to a school's social responsibilities, this issue raises the question of the emphasis placed by educational institutions on the relative importance of individual deficits *vis-à-vis* school or college deficiencies when pupils and students fail to make appropriate educational progress. The nature of the interaction of students with other students and with the educational environment provided by schools and colleges is a significant factor in learning and learning failure (Ainscow and Tweddle 1979). Various approaches to funding education, to improving standards and to making provision for those with learning difficulties, place different degrees of responsibility on pupil and school deficits.

Outcome-related funding

The funding of educational institutions is being increasingly influenced by outcome-related factors. The achievement of good results to attract increased parental and student choice is becoming a major objective. As a result of this trend, schools and colleges are paying more attention to admission policies and overt and covert forms of selection can be expected to increase. The effects of local management of schools (LMS) and the Code of Practice (DFE 1994g) will be discussed in later chapters. Except for pupils who are the subject of statements, primary and secondary schools will have to finance special educational provision from within their own budgets. Provision for students with disabilities and learning difficulties in further education was being studied at the time of writing, by a committee under the chairmanship of Professor Tomlinson, set up by the FEFC.

The crucial questions are the degree to which funding is related to institutions as a whole or to identified individuals and whether grants are solely linked to educational outcomes or take into account progress made and the value added by a school or college. A new form of payment by results will affect institutional responses to the harder to teach in the educational market. Funding linked to individuals may minimize the responsibilities of schools and colleges for the creation or exacerbation of learning difficulties. For those who work with pupils and students with disabilities and learning difficulties, this is an important issue. Outcome-related funding may result in the harder to educate being disadvantaged. Teacher persistence with learning difficulties may be discouraged. Since it may take longer to achieve a particular educational objective, costs per pupil may be higher. Competition within and between schools, while having some positive effects, may not necessarily encourage the devotion of time and resources to individual special needs. The integration of children with special educational needs may be discouraged.

This book

This book is concerned with a number of persistent and unresolved issues about the relationship of special education with primary, secondary and further education. It looks at the problems of the 'harder to teach' and the special needs which schools and colleges are expected to meet. It concentrates on a rationale for special education in the new legal framework and on the provision side of the purchaser-provider model being developed.

The independent management of schools and colleges and the increased choice of parents has created new market conditions for special educational provision. The book looks at the legal basis for provision, its definition, management, resourcing and cost effectiveness. It looks at the aspirations of the Code of Practice (DFE 1994g) and its practical implementation.

The book concludes with a possible agenda for the future management of provision to meet special educational needs in schools and colleges. This agenda identifies issues to be resolved and management tasks at all levels from central government to schools and colleges, with particular reference to the coordination of provision to meet the needs of pupils and students with disabilities and learning difficulties.

Major themes

The legislation creates a new framework for special education and work with students with disabilities and learning difficulties within a changed pattern of responsibilities for schools and colleges. The framework does not, however, resolve many of the long-standing tensions and indeed creates some new ones. Tensions between central control and local responsibility, between primary and secondary education and special education, and between the contribution of individuals and schools or colleges to learning difficulties are long standing (Audit Commission/HMI 1992a).

Many of these issues need to be reconsidered. Many continue to exist because of an inadequate dialogue between sectional interests. There are two sets of related issues, those concerning the relationship between regular and special education and those inherent in the field of special education.

Regular and special education

The first group of issues arises from the different demands and priorities of two sectors of education. They relate to the question of whether special education is considered an integral part of the education system as a whole. These issues include:

Ensuring equity in an educational market

The creation of an educational market in which individual schools and colleges compete for pupils and students is expected to result in a hierarchy of institutions based on family choices, pupil and student preferences, and National Curriculum and examination performance criteria. Although variations in performance from school to school and area to area will continue to exist, there is an expectation that standards and opportunities for choice will be similar country-wide. Parents of children with special educational needs will expect to have the same range of choice and standard of provision wherever they live. Is ensuring equity, particularly for pupils and students requiring more time and effort, a natural outcome of a free educational market?

Providing for minorities within a national framework

The national framework for education is a combination of a National Curriculum, with prescribed syllabuses, and the standardized testing of pupils at 7, 11 and 14 years of age. It is not yet clear whether the syllabuses and test procedures are sensitive to the strengths and weaknesses of minorities. Pupils with special educational needs, as currently defined, form a significant minority in most schools. The issue to be addressed is whether this approach to delivering a curriculum and assessing progress is sensitive to the educational needs of children with disabilities and learning difficulties.

Raising standards and keeping educational institutions inclusive

One of the ways to raise standards in schools and colleges is to select for admission those pupils and students who are considered most likely to be successful learners. A hierarchy of schools which select their pupils on the basis of ability and achievement may not necessarily raise general educational standards (Jonathan 1989). Some diversification of schools may be desirable for special talents and interests, for example particular arts, sciences or vocational choices. However, effective inclusive schools, which aim to recruit a balanced school population with a normal range of ability, may do more to raise the general standards of those who find it harder to learn than schools left with a population of pupils not acceptable to other schools. The issue is whether a free educational market will result in inclusive rather than exclusive schools and colleges.

Rewarding cost effectiveness without detriment to provision for the 'harder to teach'

Cost effectiveness should be the aim of all forms of education and thus is not an issue. However, there are many ways of assessing cost effectiveness (Levin 1988). Where it is defined simply in terms of end results, and takes no account of distance travelled or value added, there are real dangers. Schools may select the easy to teach with high initial achievement. Students may be put on courses well below their potential to ensure successful outcomes. The allocation of resources in schools and colleges may be skewed away from the harder to teach, where results are less predictable. Appropriate measures of cost effectiveness for the education of pupils and students with special needs are required.

Achieving quality standards where responsibilities are fragmented and provision unplanned

Until 1988 LEAs were expected to plan and manage primary, secondary, special and further education. Now, together with the FAS, they are only expected to secure and finance sufficient school places. Schools and colleges are independent contractors responsible for their own quality standards. Are parental and student choice and regular, but infrequent, inspections adequate means of ensuring appropriate national standards?

Reconciling 'absolute standards' in education (a National Curriculum and national tests) with the relative definitions of special educational needs

This is a difficult issue since it represents a conflict between two approaches to education. Up to the early 1980s, special education was an integral part of a locally planned comprehensive and inclusive system of education. The ERA 1988 created a new framework for primary and secondary education but not for special education. A competitive school and college market was created without serious discussion of its implication for special education. A National Curriculum and national attainment testing increased government influence on what was taught and how it was assessed. Increased independence for schools and colleges was linked to the measurement of pupil outcomes and a league table approach to school performance.

This idea of absolute educational standards was in marked contrast to the management of special education based on LEA-wide responsibilities and the relative definition of special educational needs and provision. This difference in approach to the attainments of all pupils and of those with special educational needs has remained a central feature of the EA 1993. There has been, as yet, no attempt to resolve it.

Reconciling administrative preoccupations with individual deficits with an acknowledgement of the role of schools in the creation of special educational needs

This issue is related to the previous one. At the time the Warnock Committee (DES 1978) was reporting, most LEAs were managing a comprehensive school system and it was recognized that schools played a significant part in the creation of some learning difficulties. This was thought particularly true of the larger group of pupils whose needs were not considered to require a statement. At that time the then Department of Education and Science (DES) chose to confine its attention to pupils with statements.

The process of making a statement tends to concentrate on pupil deficits rather than school weaknesses. The continued reliance on statements makes it important to consider how schools become aware of their own contribution to the development of learning difficulties.

Special education issues

Some issues intrinsic to special education have been made more significant by the new legislation (EA 1993). *A Code of Practice for the Identification and Assessment of Special Educational Needs* (DFE 1994g), which sets out procedures to be followed, also illuminates some issues and obscures others. It may be that a new rationale and new definitions of needs and provision will be required.

The issues which continue to be central to special education include:

What is meant by special educational needs?

It is important to recognize that the definition of special educational needs is not concerned with the conditions or circumstances which may give rise to a learning difficulty. It is concerned with what is required to enable a child with a difficulty to learn. When a medical diagnosis/ treatment model, rather than a educational one, is used, the differentiation between disabilities and difficulties and the special educational needs which arise from them presents particular problems.

Who will and should define special educational needs?

Although the Audit Commission/HMI report (1992a) called for better definitions, and many LEAs have been defining needs and levels of need more precisely, the definitions of needs in legislation and in the Code of Practice are very general. LEAs now have no powers to require schools to use the same criteria, and decisions about the existence of special educational needs will be taken by individual schools. Only when schools refer pupils for statutory assessment will the LEA be in a position to define needs and determine criteria for making statements.

The National Curriculum and standardized testing will set national standards of performance. Schools may use individual results as a basis for identifying needs but a child with special educational needs is defined as having 'a significantly greater difficulty in learning than the majority of children of his age'; or 'a disability which either prevents or hinders him from making use of educational facilities of a kind generally provided for children of his age in schools within the area of the local authority' (DFE 1993). Needs are not related to national test norms. The issue, to be discussed more fully elsewhere, is whether the Code will be effective when decision making is now so widely diffused.

What defines provision and who defines it in practice?

Is a relative definition of special educational provision practical when responsibilities are fragmented between individual schools and LEAs?

Only very general descriptions of special educational provision exist. All too often provision is implicitly defined by location (a special school or unit) or by personnel (the existence of teachers with special education training and experience) (Fish 1989). Although individual statements may define provision more precisely, there is little agreement about the arrangements that primary and secondary schools might be expected to make for pupils whose needs do not require a statement. Because many in education do not distinguish between good education and special education, schools may need clearer guidance about what is and is not special educational provision.

How can unlimited demands and parental choice be reconciled with economic realities and limited resources?

Resources for special education are finite and it is necessary that their use is cost effective. The new framework disperses existing funds more widely. The monitoring of the effective use of resources available to meet special educational needs will be sporadic at best. LEAs will be faced with many demands for the use of retained funds. Meeting parental wishes and responding to the decisions of the new Tribunals (EA 1993: Part III) may make it difficult for them to develop a coherent policy for securing provision. The main issue is whether choice and the effective management of resources can be developed within the new framework.

Perspectives

There are many more interested parties and professions with points of view and vested interests in special education, than in primary, secondary and further education. These different perspectives need to be borne in mind as each of the major themes is discussed. The competition for the attention and resources of the many different interests involved has always made it difficult for LEAs to plan and manage special educational provision.

Parents' choice of school is a central feature of educational policy. The views of parents and families on special educational provision, as well as those of their children as they get older, are now particularly important. Parental rights have been increased and their rights to appeal to an independent Tribunal enshrined in law.

Voluntary organizations have always played an important role in raising awareness of needs. Many have pioneered new forms of provision. Together with parents and families, they have campaigned for the best arrangements for particular forms of disability. In one sense, voluntary organizations have been the forerunners of a special education market as they have competed for attention and for funds to meet the needs of children, young people and adults with particular disabilities and learning difficulties. While policies and planning can be improved by the contributions of parents and voluntary organizations, they can also be distorted by well-organized campaigns and strongly expressed preferences, as research in Scotland has shown (Riddell *et al.* 1994).

The attitudes and knowledge of the **staff of mainstream schools and colleges** are very significant in the early detection of such needs. Most of the less severe special educational needs first manifest themselves in schools. The development of needs may also be influenced by teachers' ability to manage different rates and styles of learning. The attitudes and effectiveness of the staff of primary and secondary schools and their use of resources can influence the incidence of special educational needs and the extent to which they are adequately met in those schools.

Educational psychologists and advisory and support teachers have played, and continue to play, an important role in establishing the nature and severity of special educational needs. They have also provided help and support to teachers with such children in their classes. Their perspectives will be influenced by both professional and employer interests but they are essential to effective assessment and programme planning for individuals with special educational needs.

Staff with direct responsibilities for special educational provision may work in special schools, units and other forms of provision. Their constant interaction with pupils with special educational needs gives them an important perspective on provision, particularly the effectiveness of different practices and methodologies. When circumstances and resources allow, they also provide important support to the staff of regular schools and colleges. However, many have a vested interest in the kind of provision the schools and colleges make and their knowledge and experience of primary, secondary and further education are not always extensive.

Local educational administrators are particularly concerned with special education regulations, the administration of procedures for assessment and making statements. They need to understand the relationship between regular and special education, work within finite budgets and deal with a wide range of parental, school and voluntary group demands. Until a common funding formula for schools is agreed, LEA administrators have powers to structure the use of resources for special education, including those delegated to schools through Local Management of Schools (LMS) and Local Management of Special Schools (LMSS) formulae. In many ways, the perspective of administrators is wider and better informed than others concerned with special education. However, the potential to plan and manage provision is now more limited. The formulation of well-planned purchasing policies may be all that is possible.

Considerable indirect influence on provision can be exercised by **the Office for Standards in Education (Ofsted), the Audit Commission, and the funding agencies (FAS and FEFC)** through reports and fiscal policies. Much depends on the priority accorded to special education within the Department for Education (DFE), FAS and HM Inspectorate. Decisions about this aspect of education tend to be taken as a consequence of other policy decisions. Many of the major issues outlined in this book stem from an inability to consider special education as an integral element of national education policies from the outset.

Another perspective which influences special education, is that of the many **professional associations and unions**, members of which contribute to provision. In some respects, they represent another market of competing claims. However, at their best, effective associations and unions have a constructive influence on meeting special educational needs.

When **local and national politicians** are well informed about special education, they can make important contributions to developments. However, their perspective is often influenced by particular cases and by their association with voluntary organizations. Emotional support for special education is often strong, but a detailed understanding of its nature is less common.

A final but most important perspective is provided by **those with disabilities and learning difficulties** (Booth *et al.* 1992; Wade and Moore 1993). Self-advocacy skills have been improved through voluntary organizations and the formation of disability groups. Much more attention is being paid to their experiences, concerns and views. The Code of Practice stresses the importance of listening to the views of children and young people about their needs, and effective transition programmes to develop self-advocacy skills.

Conclusion

Subsequent chapters will argue that a new rationale for special educational provision is necessary. Those concerned with special education have continued to support the philosophy and approach of the Warnock Report (DES 1978) and the 1981 Education Act (DES 1981); but subsequent legislation has created a competitive educational market. As yet, there has been no attempt by the DFE to reconcile special educational policy with a market approach.

The different special educational needs being identified, the nature of provision, and the range of facilities and services necessary to meet them are ill-defined. It is the purpose of this book to look at the way special educational provision may be expected to develop, to consider how it may be managed when provided by semi-independent contractors, and to identify the many uncertainties which require resolution.

2 / The New Framework

Two Education Acts passed in the early 1990s (FHEA 1992 and EA 1993) are statements of confidence in an educational market and a restatement of responsibilities. Both Acts redefine responsibilities for providing education for children with disabilities and learning difficulties. Discontinuities are created because in the 16–19 age range, where both Acts apply, schools and further education institutions with different regulations and funding mechanisms, compete for students. Nevertheless the two Acts together with the Code of Practice, are important starting points from which to consider the future management of special education facilities and services for pupils and students. This chapter is concerned with the substance of the two Acts and with the Code of Practice.

Needs and provision

A number of priorities recognized in earlier government policies are reaffirmed by the Acts. They solve some long-standing problems, leave others unresolved and have the potential to create future difficulties. With respect to special education, the importance of individual special education programmes is recognized as is the need for effective early intervention and for post-school provision. However, definitions of needs vary with the EA 1993 referring to pupils with special educational needs and the FHEA 1992 to students with disabilities and learning difficulties.

One of the outstanding characteristics of recent decades has been the concentration on assessment and the establishment of new types of need. During the same period, the skills of special education teachers have increased and services to support the work of class and subject teachers in primary and secondary schools have developed. More recently, there has been increased emphasis on the use of statements to earmark scarce resources. The nature of the range of provision necessary to meet special educational needs has received only limited attention and there is little evidence about the effectiveness of the different forms of special education.

Choice and the market

Prior to recent legislation, market forces in special education had been limited to competition between voluntary and special interest groups. These groups have established needs and contributed a great deal to provision. Many voluntary organizations have also competed for attention and public funds. Rival campaigning claims have often made it difficult for both central and local government to establish a balanced range of provision and an equitable and effective use of available resources.

The purchaser-provider model is being introduced into special education as part of a general education market. But there is considerable uncertainty about who is a purchaser and who is a provider, and the nature of the division between the two. Parental choice is now seen as paramount. Parents of children with special educational needs now have more choice of provision and can appeal to an independent tribunal if they are dissatisfied with LEA proposals.

The Education Reform Act 1988

Before turning to the 1990 Acts, it is necessary to recognize the main provisions of the ERA 1988. This established a National Curriculum and a national system of attainment testing at the ages of 7, 11 and 14. It reduced the powers and duties of LEAs by introducing the local management of schools (LMS). LEAs had to delegate a wide range of management responsibilities, including responsibility for a school's budget, to school governors.

The ERA 1988 set up a new type of school, the grant-maintained (GM) school, to be directly funded from the centre, in the first instance by the DFE. Both primary and secondary schools could apply for this status, which had to be approved by the Secretary of State. There turned out to be a number of serious limitations in the ERA 1988 which necessitated the introduction of the 1993 legislation (EA 1993).

The Further and Higher Education Act 1992

The FHEA 1992 granted polytechnics and some colleges of higher education university status. All institutions solely catering for young people over the compulsory school age of 16 (colleges of further education, tertiary and Sixth Form colleges) were made independent institutions. They were given their own non-elected and self-perpetuating Boards of Management. A Further Education Funding Council (FEFC) was set up to manage and finance the sector.

The FHEA 1992 makes the FEFC responsible for ensuring that provision is made for students with disabilities and learning difficulties. Post-school education for these students will be discussed more fully in Chapter 7. At this stage it is important to note that this is the first legal recognition of post-school educational provision for young people with disabilities and learning difficulties.

The Education Act 1993

The EA 1993 considerably increased the powers of the Secretary of State for Education. Part I is concerned with a Funding Agency for Schools (FAS), responsibilities for schools and other matters; Part II deals with grant-maintained schools; Part III with special education; Part IV with attendance; Part V with schools failing to give an acceptable standard of education and Part VI with miscellaneous matters.

The FAS is made responsible for the financing of grant-maintained schools. Part I also deals with the Secretary of State's powers to make the FAS responsible for securing educational provision in certain circumstances. The FAS is jointly responsible with an LEA when not less than 10 per cent of the school population is in grant-maintained schools and wholly responsible when the percentage is 75 or more. Both the LEA and the FAS are given powers to direct the admission of pupils to schools.

Part II deals with grant-maintained schools, the achievement of grant-maintained status and the establishment of new schools. It is made possible for special schools to gain grant-maintained status and the FAS can set up such schools in prescribed circumstances. Two or more grant-maintained schools can enter a joint scheme of management. Further sections deal with grants and changes of character of schools.

Part III is a major restatement of special education legislation. It updates the definitions of the 1981 Education Act and confirms the duties of LEAs. It also introduces the Code of Practice giving guidance about the discharge of functions. A significant new feature is the requirement that governors of LEA-maintained and grant-maintained nursery, primary and secondary schools should secure provision to meet special educational needs which are not the subject of statements. Schools are to make annual reports to parents in a prescribed form giving information about the school's policy for identifying and meeting special educational needs and how the policy is to be implemented.

The LEA may provide services to both LEA-maintained and grant-maintained schools in their areas or elsewhere, which can be charged for under prescribed conditions. Services must be provided free to both kinds of school when required for statutory assessment or when specified in a child's statement. Part III restates statutory assessment procedures, first introduced by the 1981 Education Act, with new time limits and new appeal procedures which include the setting up of a Special Educational Tribunal. Further sections deal with special schools, the approval of independent schools and non-maintained special schools.

The major changes introduced for special education are the Code of Practice and the Appeals Tribunal but the EA 1993 is an important milestone in other ways. It is the first legislation to make nursery, primary and secondary schools of all kinds responsible for meeting special educational needs. It also restates LEA responsibilities for special education and gives them powers to obtain information from other schools and agencies to enable them to carry out their duties.

The Code of Practice

A Code of Practice for the Identification and Assessment of Special Educational Needs (DFE 1994g) is now described in some detail because it is the framework, provided by the DFE, for future practices and provision.

Foreword

The Foreword to the Code stresses that schools and LEAs must have regard to the Code but recognizes that 'having regard' may vary according to school circumstances over time.

Section 1

Section 1 of the Code stresses *integration, intervention* and *partnership*. It sets out the fundamental principles on which it is based. The Code recognizes that:

- there is a continuum of needs and a continuum of provision, which may be made in a wide variety of forms;
- children with special educational needs should have the maximum possible access to the National Curriculum;
- the needs of most pupils will be met in mainstream schools and, taking into account the wishes of parents, children will be educated alongside their peers in mainstream schools;
- even before compulsory school age a child may have educational needs requiring the intervention of the LEA as well as the health service;
- effective assessment and provision will be secured where there is the greatest possible degree of partnership between parents and their children and schools, LEAs and other agencies.

Section 1 of the Code goes on to state that provision for special educational needs should be made by the most appropriate agency, most commonly the child's mainstream school. In most cases, where mainstream schools work in partnership with the child's parents, no statutory assessment will be necessary.

Where necessary, an LEA must make assessments setting out the child's educational and non-educational needs, the provision to be made and the arrangements for monitoring and reviewing them. What is meant by 'non-educational needs' is not specified.

It is emphasized that special educational provision will be most effective when those responsible take into account the ascertainable wishes of the child concerned, considered in the light of his or her understanding.

The Code states that the overriding interest of all concerned is to ensure that appropriate provision is made for children with special educational needs. The ordering of the guidance reflects the particular conditions affecting the 'treatment' of children at different stages in their lives and school careers. The reference to 'treatment' is a reversion to the language of the 1944 Education Act and to a medical model for provision.

Section 2

Section 2 of the Code sets out definitions, the responsibilities of governors and the school-based stages of assessment and provision.

Definitions

This section of the Code sets out the definitions of special educational needs and provision in the EA 1993. The EA 1993 definition of provision for a child under two, is 'educational provision of any kind'. For a child over two, it is 'educational provision which is additional to, or otherwise different from, the educational provision made generally for children of the child's age in maintained schools other than special schools'.

Governors

School governing bodies have a statutory duty to ensure that the special educational needs of the majority of children are met. The governing body must:

- do their best to secure that the necessary provision is made for any pupil with special educational needs;
- make annual reports to parents in a prescribed form giving details of the school's policy for identifying and meeting special educational needs and how that policy is being implemented.

It is the responsibility of each school governing body to decide how best to provide for children with special educational needs and the Code and regulations set out what must be included in a policy statement.

The governing body's annual report to parents should state the number of pupils with SEN and demonstrate the effectiveness of the school's systems for identification, assessment, provision, monitoring and record keeping and specify the use made of outside support services and agencies. Governors have to ensure that the school has a SEN coordinator. Further sections of the Code set out the duties of SEN coordinators. There is no indication of the experience and training necessary for governors and SEN coordinators nor of the time required to carry out the specified duties.

Assessment

The Code goes on to set out procedures for three stages of school-based assessment. The proposed stages are essentially the same as those outlined in the Warnock Report (DES 1978).

At **Stage 1**, the trigger is concern about a child's progress and behaviour in school based on appropriate class-teacher evidence for that concern. Assessment procedures must include the involvement of parents, where possible the involvement of pupils, and liaison with other agencies. At the end of Stage 1, those concerned must decide whether to continue current arrangements, to seek further advice or to draw up an education plan using expertise within the school. If an individual education plan is to be drawn up it must set out:

- curricular needs (precise curriculum priorities, learning objectives and criteria for success, and monitoring and recording arrangements);
- teaching requirements (teaching strategies, techniques, equipment and materials);
- non-curricular needs (pastoral care arrangements and medical requirements);
- review arrangements (review date, always within a term, and the people to be involved).

The child moves to **Stage 2** if, after two reviews at Stage 1, the class teacher and SEN coordinator decide that the individual education plans have not resulted in the child making satisfactory progress.

At Stage 2, the SEN coordinator takes the lead in assessing the child's learning difficulties. The trigger is either a Stage 1 review decision or, when concern first arises, the SEN coordinator's judgement that intensive intervention is necessary. On the basis of available information the SEN coordinator decides to seek further advice and/or draw up a new education plan. The plan at this stage should set out needs, requirements and arrangements under the same headings as Stage 1. Under teaching requirements, three additional sections have to be completed:

- the staff involved;
- the size of teaching group;
- the frequency and timing of support.

Stage 3 involves external specialist support. The trigger is either unsatisfactory Stage 2 reviews or the need, recognized at the outset, for external support. At this stage, the SEN coordinator decides to seek further advice from other agencies and/or to draw up a new education plan including the involvement of other agencies. The plan, at this stage, should set out needs requirements and arrangements under the same headings as Stages 1 and 2. An additional section, under teaching requirements, has to be completed specifying the nature of external support.

The SEN coordinator should convene three review meetings to assess progress and the effectiveness of the individual plan and to decide on future action. The courses open are to continue at Stage 3, to revert to Stage 2 or to refer to the LEA for statutory assessment. Such referrals, made on the basis of the SEN coordinator's reports, should be endorsed by a responsible person (for example, headteacher, governor or chairman of governors).

Provision

In the first three stages, provision is seen in terms of individual education plans. The school's role in collecting and recording information and reviewing progress is specified in detail. Parameters of the plan are specified, but there is no indication of the nature or extent of the provision schools of different sizes and types might be expected to make. Although contributions by external facilities and services to individual plans are recognized, there is no indication of the nature of the services on which schools may expect to call or who is responsible for their provision or quality.

Although the proposed stages are essentially the same as those proposed by the Warnock Report, little account appears to have been taken of experience in their use since that time. The emphasis on individual education plans and on the involvement of parents and pupils in assessment is very constructive. The resource implications – in terms of class teacher and SEN coordinator time required to carry out procedures, to prepare evidence, to write reports and to work with parents in schools of different sizes and types – are not recognized. The use of the word 'provision' almost always refers to the putting into effect of individual education programmes (that is, the arrangements to be made for the individual). There is little reference to the range of facilities and services from which individual education programmes might be developed or to the general school planning and ethos which might mitigate or create special educational needs.

Section 3

Section 3 of the Code sets out procedures for the statutory assessment of special educational needs. The legislation and the Code make LEAs responsible for identifying and making a statutory assessment of those children who have special educational needs and probably need a statement. The Section describes how children may be brought to the attention of LEAs, the procedures they should follow, the time limits within which assessments and statements should be made and criteria for making statutory assessments. LEAs are expected to write to schools 'periodically' to find out how many pupils are at Stage 3. It is also suggested that LEAs set up moderating groups to develop and apply criteria.

Criteria should include academic attainments. This is particularly important where there may be significant discrepancies between either a child's attainments in assessments and tests in core subjects and the attainments of the majority of children of the same age, or between National Curriculum test results and the performance expected of the child, as indicated by a consensus of those teaching and observing him or her. Criteria should also include significant discrepancies within one core subject or between one core subject and another. The LEA should seek evidence about the effects of health, sensory impairment, attendance, home problems and emotional and behaviour difficulties. Further paragraphs set out the case for provision and give guidance about the nature of learning difficulties, emotional and behaviour difficulties, physical disabilities, specific learning difficulties, sensory impairments and medical conditions.

Because of the relativity of special educational needs, specific criteria are not defined, but in each case statutory assessment should be considered when associated learning difficulties:

- are significant and/or complex;
- have not responded to relevant and purposeful measures;
- may call for provision not reasonably provided within mainstream school budgets and/or require continuing oversight by the LEA.

The detailed guidance assumes that LEAs will establish criteria in their own areas and that all schools will have trained and experienced SEN staff. The Code provides many potential grounds for dispute between schools and the LEA. The latter can refer individuals back to schools for further information and schools will have to be very efficient to make an acceptable case for statutory assessment.

Section 4

Section 4 of the Code is concerned with statements. Having made a statutory assessment, LEAs then have to decide whether to make a statement. The Code sets out the main criteria which are that:

- necessary provision cannot be made within the resources available to schools;
- the LEA concludes that it must determine all provision in order to ensure continuing oversight of provision.

In coming to a decision LEAs might ask, in respect of the child's learning difficulties, whether the evidence of assessment is in accord with evidence from the school, or whether there are aspects of the difficulties which have been overlooked and which, with advice, equipment and other provision, could be effectively addressed by the school within its own resources. LEAs should also show that the school's approaches were appropriate and if not, whether there are appropriate approaches which could, with advice and support, be adopted by the school within its own resources.

The LEA may conclude that the school is able to make provision which includes occasional specialist advice, occasional non-teaching support, minor pieces of equipment and minor adaptations to buildings. But if the child requires regular direct specialist teaching, daily individual non-teaching support, significant equipment, major building adaptations, a change of placement including day or residential special school placement then a statement should be considered.

The Code and Regulations specify that a statement should be made in six parts. Part I should set out details about the child and the family. Part II must set out the details of the child's special educational needs identified by the statutory assessment. Part III of the statement should specify the objectives which special educational provision should aim to meet, the provision which the LEA considers appropriate to meet the needs specified in Part II, and the arrangements for monitoring and review. Part IV of the statement is concerned with placement and parts V and VI with 'non-educational' needs and the 'non-educational' provision which the LEA is expected to agree with other agencies.

The LEA must draw up the proposed statement completing all parts except Part IV, which must be left blank so that the LEA does not pre-empt parental choice. The proposed statement must not contain any suggestion about where the proposed special educational provision should be made. Parental choice and other negotiations about placement are expected to be completed in a period of eight weeks between the proposed and final statement.

Although assessment at Stages 1 to 3 of the Code is expected to result in an individual education plan, statutory assessment at Stages 4 and 5 is still seen as specifying LEA/professional objectives. The distinction between the objectives of provision and the means of achieving them through individual education programmes is not recognized at this stage. There is no apparent requirement for the statement process to end with an individual education plan.

Section 5

Section 5 of the Code is concerned with assessment and statements for children under five. The section restates the legal position and suggests that special needs will first be recognized by child health services. Assessment should take place where the child and the family feel comfortable. Statements for children under the age of two will be rare. Any intervention will require close collaboration with health services.

For children under five, LEAs should consider providing guidance on recording progress to those providing for young children and work closely with health and social services. The information necessary as a basis for assessment and making a statement is specified but criteria for making statements are not. There is useful advice on the exchange of information between pre-school facilities and primary schools.

Section 6

Section 6 of the Code deals with annual reviews of children with statements. It sets out the aims of reviews. The first paragraphs deal with reviews before the child reaches the age of 14. The LEA will require headteachers to submit reports by a specified date giving at least two months' notice. Before producing the report the headteacher must convene a meeting to discuss its contents and must circulate a summary of advice before the meeting. The LEA initiates the review and concludes it, but most of the process is school based. Later paragraphs describe procedures for 14+ reviews including the requirement for translation and actions following the review.

Annual reviews during the 14–16 age range are dealt with separately. This section recognizes the transition phase and process, the relevance of other legislation and the involvement of other agencies. LEAs are responsible for conducting these reviews.

Review procedures place another burden on schools and the Code does not recognize the time and resource implications of the expected procedures. The acknowledgement of the importance of transition is a positive step, but whether LEAs and other agencies will have the resources to make their contributions to a coordinated plan is uncertain.

Conclusion

The EA 1993 statutory regulations and the Code of Practice (DFE 1994g) set out the future framework for special education. It is a combination of requirements and aspirations which builds on earlier legislation. The Code says more about identifying and assessing needs than meeting them. The resource implications of the school-based assessment and provision expected by the new framework have not yet been seriously considered. At the time the legislation was passed, it was said to be 'resource neutral'. There appears to be an unrealistic assumption that adequate resources exist and that all that is required is good management. The government appears to be relying on well-informed and active consumers to monitor the effectiveness of the Code.

3 / Perspectives in 1993

A considerable amount of evidence and opinion about special education became available in 1992–3. This included reports such as that of the Audit Commission and HMI *Getting in on the Act* (1992a), evidence to the House of Commons Education Committee enquiry into the use of statements (House of Commons 1993) and submissions about provision in the Bill which became the Education Act 1993 (EA 1993). Although the terms of reference for the various enquiries were different, the submissions had much in common. This chapter presents and evaluates the perspectives on special education which were put into the public arena in the early 1990s.

The Audit Commission and HMI report

The Audit Commission and HMI report *Getting in on the Act* was based on a detailed study of the 1981 Act procedures in twelve LEAs and discussions in many more. It was looking for economy, efficiency and effectiveness in the provision of special education. It concluded that much had been achieved since the Act was implemented, and that the principles upon which it was based were widely endorsed. A companion report: *Getting the Act Together* (Audit Commission/HMI 1992b) gave examples of the successful implementation of every major provision of the 1981 Act. The reports stated that it was the operation of the Act by LEAs which was problematic, not its principles.

Getting in on the Act concluded that there was no consistent definition of what is meant by 'special educational needs'. This resulted in a lack of clarity, accountability and incentives for those attempting to make provision. Among other recommendations, the Report suggested:

- the need for a framework for defining the responsibilities of primary and secondary schools for provision;
- the use of special needs performance indicators at school level;
- that the use of statements should continue but that the DFE should issue guidance about the levels of need which should trigger the statutory assessment procedures;
- that there should be time limits for the completion of assessments;
- that a new type of statement should specify objectives and resources;
- that consideration should be given to the use of financial incentives to persuade LEAs to implement fully the 1981 Act.

The Report concluded that the basic principles of the 1981 Act were capable of operation and that in future, a 'purchaser/provider' model should be implemented with LEAs purchasing and schools providing special education.

Markets, Competition and Vulnerability (Evans and Lunt 1994), argues that:

> These documents highlight the difficulties inherent in trying to protect the interests of vulnerable children in a system where accountability and responsibility are already diffuse and are becoming more so. *Getting in on the Act* rightly highlights these problems but the solutions proposed are merely administrative and lack any organising principle which would protect the interests of pupils with SEN, since the over-riding objective is to uphold the principles of maximum delegation to schools and relies on systems of accountability which are, as yet, untested.
>
> (pp. 13–14)

House of Commons Education Committee Report

The House of Commons Education Committee collected a wide range of evidence about the operation of the 1981 Act during 1992–3. The Third Report of the Committee (House of Commons 1993) stated that:

> There is concern about many aspects of special educational needs, such as assessment procedures (from which statements might result) and a considerable amount of evidence is available about the

> subject. However, in our enquiry we have decided to concentrate on the use of statements, their purposes and the children for the provision of whom they might be necessary, together with the implications for special education of the Education Bill at present before Parliament.
>
> (p. xiii, para. 5)

Written evidence was sought on nine aspects of the subject, including whether statements were a useful and cost-effective way of allocating resources and what changes might be necessary to reflect the 'purchaser/provider' model. Other topics were: the criteria for making statements; the special educational needs for which primary and secondary schools would be responsible; and the definition, financing and evaluation of provision. Evidence was sought on variations between LEAs in percentages of pupils with statements and the extent to which LEAs should provide centrally funded support services. Questions were also asked about parental choice and whether steps were necessary to ensure equity in the face of expensive individual parent demands.

Issues for special education

The opinions and evidence put forward in 1993 form the basis for this chapter. They are primarily concerned with the working of the 1981 Act, the preparation and use of statements and the proposals in the 1993 Education Bill then being enacted. The various submissions provide a starting point for a consideration of the issues facing special education at the time, many of which continue to require attention. These issues, many of which will be discussed in detail in later chapters, can be conveniently grouped under the following headings:

- Responsibilities of primary and secondary schools for SEN;
  for support services to school;
  for children with statements (the '2%') and without statements (the '18%');
- Prevalence of special educational needs;
- Criteria for statutory assessment;
  for making statements;
- Administration LEA responsibilities;
  FAS responsibilities;
  the role of governors;
  local government reorganization;
  bureaucracy and the market model;
  the 'purchaser-provider' model;
  the role of Tribunals;

- Finance — accountability and incentives;
  demands and LEA budgets;
  payment for support services;
- Training — training for local management;
  training and the nature of provision;
- Inter-agency collaboration and coordination;
- Parental choice — appeals;
  advocacy and equity;
  limits;
  children's views.

Responsibilities

School responsibilities

When the ERA 1988 was passed, there was an assumption that primary and secondary schools would be responsible for meeting the needs of pupils who were experiencing the less severe and complex learning difficulties and who were not provided with statements. However, the delegation of increased powers (including admission policies) to school governing bodies, and the decrease in powers of the LEAs to manage educational provision, resulted in considerable uncertainty about the relative responsibilities of LEAs and schools. The evidence given to the House of Commons Committee by the Council for Disabled Children (CDC) summarizes them. When commenting on which children should be provided with statements, the CDC stated:

> We are conscious, from the evidence of our members, that the debate about statementing has, in some instances, obscured the wider need to:
>
> (i) Clarify the responsibilities of individual schools to identify and meet special educational needs within existing resources before deciding to seek additional support.
> (ii) Ensure that LEAs develop and apply formulae as required by the 1988 Act which adequately reflect the incidence of pupils with special educational needs within ordinary schools . . .

The CDC further commented that:

> It is not clear:
>
> (i) How the LEA will implement its duties in grant-maintained schools, where it may place and fund children with special educational needs, but has currently no formal rights on entry or scrutiny.
> (ii) How the LEA and the Funding Agency will work concurrently

> in ensuring that there are sufficient and appropriate school places in order to meet special needs for which the LEA will be the 'purchaser' . . .
>
> (House of Commons 1993: vol. II, p. 29)

These were very real concerns at the time. The 1993 Act and the Code of Practice deal with responsibilities but there remain many areas of uncertainty about criteria and provision. These will be discussed in more detail in Chapter 5.

Support services

In the years following the Warnock Report and the 1981 Act, most LEAs reorganized and developed a range of psychological and support teaching services to schools (Goacher *et al.* 1988). These services were sometimes disability specific, for example, for hearing impairment, and sometimes generic, that is, concerned with all special educational needs. The functions of most services were to help schools identify and assess learning difficulties, to support the educational provision the school made, and to help primary and secondary school teachers meet more special educational needs within their schools. Considerable progress was made in the development of more effective services up to the end of the 1980s.

The implementation of local management of schools (LMS) brought changes to the ways in which support for schools was organized and funded. The requirement on LEAs to delegate a significant and increasing percentage of their budget to individual schools led to a decrease in funding for central services and corresponding cuts to SEN support services. The evidence of the extent of the cuts is equivocal (NUT/Spastics Society 1993; Evans *et al.* 1994a), but services felt under pressure.

LEAs are responsible for provision for pupils with statements. However, responsibilities for services for the larger group of pupils whose needs are not the subject of statements, remain unclear. Evidence to the House of Commons Education Committee (HOC 1993) suggested that most schools would not have sufficient expertise for all needs and would continue to require psychological and support teaching services of all kinds. It was also thought that most school budgets would not be sufficient to allow for the purchase of such services. At the same time, the continued existence of support services was said to be an important element in maintaining an adequate range of special educational provision.

The evidence was much less clear about the kinds of services which might be necessary, although services for sensory impairment were thought to be essential by most of those who gave evidence on this topic. There was less unanimity about services for other types of learning and behaviour difficulties. Doubt was cast by some witnesses on the quality and effectiveness of these services in some LEAs. There was also little factual evidence of the size of services necessary for particular functions. As in other areas of special education, data about cost-effectiveness was limited. These issues will be looked at again in the light of current legislation in later chapters.

Prevalence of special educational needs

Two proportions, indicated in the Warnock Report (DES 1978), are commonly used to describe the prevalence of special educational needs: 2 per cent for children with statements and 18 per cent for children with needs not requiring a statement. In practice, accurate figures have only been collected for the proportion of children with statements. These vary between just over 1 per cent to over 4 per cent in different LEAs. The Audit Commission/HMI (1992a) and Audit Commission (1994) noted a lack of clarity in the specification of needs requiring a statement, but while needs continue to be defined as relative to the performance of other children in a school or area (see Chapter 1), precise national criteria for the provision of statements may be impossible. This view was echoed by the House of Commons Education Committee report which stated: 'There is . . . no distinct and defined population of children to whom the (1981) Act applies.' (HOC 1993: p. xiv, para. 10).

The increase in statement percentages reported after the implementation of LMS reflected two major resourcing problems. These were limited school budgets and uncertainty about the size and use of the special education element within those budgets (Evans and Lunt 1994). As a result, parents and schools were seeking to obtain statements for children in order to obtain additional resources.

'Objective' data, such as that obtained from national tests, may not help to define the size of the population of pupils with special educational needs, since it would be uncertain how far individual pupil performance was due to school factors rather than 'within child' factors. A number of constructive approaches to the identification of the extent of special educational needs and the resourcing requirements of different levels and types of need emerged from the evidence to the House of Commons Committee. These included the banding system used by Leeds LEA, the resource allocation system used by Nottinghamshire LEA, and the individual school audit practised by Kent LEA. These will be looked at in more detail in Chapter 6.

Criteria for making statements

An area of concern to those giving evidence to the House of Commons Education Committee was the criteria being used to initiate statutory assessment and to make a statement. The position is exemplified in the evidence of the Council for Disabled Children (CDC) which stated:

> There has been considerable national debate about the 'threshold' for formal Section 5 assessment under the current 1981 Education Act. Whilst we are aware that rigid criteria are probably unworkable, given the widely varying nature of local provision and individual children's needs, we strongly recommend that there should be wide consultation about a clear national framework for assessment . . .
>
> (HOC 1993: vol. II, p. 29, para. 3a)

These views were echoed in much of the evidence. The National Curriculum Council suggested that criteria should be linked to national test results and the Audit Commission appeared to think that more objective criteria should be developed. The House of Commons Education Committee Report stated:

> The original purpose of the statement was to safeguard provision for pupils with severe, long term special educational needs. It was to identify and record needs and specify provision to meet them. Much of the evidence we received suggests that the original intentions have not always been realised in local education authority policies and practices and that later legislation and resource limitations have affected the purposes for which statements are made. A clarification is needed in the process by which LEAs decide whether or not to make statements. We recommend that the DFE, in its Code of Practice, provide criteria and guidelines for LEAs, to assist them to decide, having assessed a child, when they need to make a statement of a child's special educational needs.
>
> (HOC 1993: p. xix, para. 25)

The Code now exists, setting out detailed guidelines for stages of assessment but avoiding the specification of national criteria. It recommends that LEAs set up moderating committees to develop local criteria. There is a potential for disagreement between schools and LEAs at Stage 4 of the Code's assessment procedures, the initiation of statutory assessment, because the Code's guidelines are capable of different interpretations. It cannot be said that the DFE, through the Code of Practice, has taken positive steps to deal with the question of national criteria for provision of a statement. That this is an on-going problem is confirmed by the latest Audit Commission *Bulletin* which noted that: 'guidelines on the threshold of needs that warrants instigation of the process of formal assessment . . . need to be developed urgently' (Audit Commission 1994: 20).

The administration of special education

Legislation, including the EA 1993, reaffirmed LEAs' responsibilities for special education policy development. In particular, these were to carry out statutory assessments, to make statements (where appropriate), and to secure the provision specified in statements. At the same time, the proportion of the education budget to be managed by schools was increased and the influence of LEAs over schools, in which special educational needs arise and from whom requests for assessment come, was much reduced. Planning for a range of provision and services was made increasingly difficult. The possibility of local government reorganization was another factor which led to an uncertain environment for LEAs.

The relative responsibilities of LEAs and the FAS were also a matter for concern. When the percentage of pupils being educated in grant-maintained (GM) primary or secondary schools is such that the FAS becomes responsible for provision in an area, the LEA remains responsible for special education. However, the FAS can sanction the provision of GM special schools, thus further fragmenting the planning of provision. This was an issue raised before the House of Commons Education Committee by a number of witnesses. The effects of an educational market, based on parental choice and competing schools, on the management of special educational provision was not taken into account by the government at the time the legislation was passed. Nor was the nature of the purchaser/provider model for LEA special education responsibilities clearly spelt out. Although the EA 1993 has clarified certain issues, there remains concern about planning an appropriate range of provision where duties and responsibilities are fragmented. According to the government and DFE witnesses to the House of Commons Education Committee, market forces and good communication were seen to be all that was necessary (HOC 1993: vol. II, pp. 188–96 and appendix 15, pp. 225–6).

Financing special education

Two themes – the reality of finite resources and the unlimited aspirations of parents, professionals and voluntary organizations – ran counter to each other in evidence to the House of Commons Education Committee. LEA officers recognized that finances were finite. Most other evidence barely acknowledged resource limitations and insisted that all identified needs should be met. As the Committee's report comments:

> With finite resources, this leads to difficulties in practice. First, any increase in resources for statements reduces the funding generally available to schools, including that to meet the wider range of SENs.

> Secondly, if more statements are produced, the funding available to resource each statement may be reduced.
>
> (HOC 1993: vol. I, p. xvii, para. 31)

The financing of special education in the future is discussed in Chapter 8.

Training issues

For some years, the DES, subsequently the DFE, had been targeting funds for teacher training on departmental priorities. One of these was the training of teachers in primary and secondary schools to be SEN coordinators. The subsequent introduction of the National Curriculum moved priorities and funding away from SEN training towards preparation for the introduction of the National Curriculum.

At the time the EA 1993 was implemented, it was not clear how many schools had SEN coordinators with appropriate training. Nor was it known how many of the numerous non-teaching assistants (NTAs) supporting special educational provision had received any training. The training implications of the EA 1993 and the Code of Practice for teachers and non-teaching assistants were not specified. Nor were there any requirements that teachers and assistants delivering 'special education' should have any training. The effective implementation of the new framework requires an adequately funded training policy.

Inter-agency collaboration

Adequate provision for children with severe and complex physical, sensory and intellectual disabilities often requires contributions from health and social services as well as from education services. For many years, different agencies have been encouraged to work together, but different planning cycles, financial priorities and target groups have made this difficult in practice (Goacher *et al.* 1988). The EA 1993 and the Code of Practice require other agencies to assist with assessment and provision, but this requirement is qualified with the proviso of 'effective use of resources'. The Children Act 1989 (DoH 1989) has a similar requirement for 'children with special needs', but different definitions and requirements across agencies make collaboration difficult to achieve.

Parents

The last theme running through the evidence in 1993 was the greater participation of parents in choosing education for their children and the need for more independent appeal procedures. Both these issues were addressed in the EA 1993 and the Code of Practice.

A number of concerns were expressed about the effects of parental choice on an educational market, especially when children had less acceptable forms of special educational needs. There has always been a 'pecking order' of special educational needs, with moderate learning difficulties and emotional and behaviour problems at the bottom of the order. One of the problems brought to the attention of the House of Commons Committee was the effect of powerful advocacy by a minority of parents on behalf of their children on the provision possible for others. The question of appropriate advocacy for the needs of some children and equity in provision for others cannot be avoided. The claims of pupils with special educational needs versus those of average and above average ability must also be addressed. It is doubtful whether these competing claims for resources will be solved by a 'market' approach (Bowe *et al.* 1992).

Conclusion

At the stage at which the House of Commons Committee conducted its enquiry, it was possible to see that Government attention was focused on the individual, and not on the system of special education. If needs were specified in a statement and if an individual programme was devised, then provision was simply a matter of finding a school where it could be made. Special educational provision appeared to be envisaged as an accumulation of individual programmes. The range of facilities and services necessary before programmes could be put into effect was receiving little attention. As the following chapters will show, this approach has its limitations.

4 / Basic Issues and Policy Development

This chapter looks briefly at the historical background to current issues and the implications of previous legislation and of the Warnock Report (DES 1978). This report stressed the importance of both a planned range of educational provision to meet a range of needs and a continuity of provision from the early years to adulthood. The effects of subsequent policies on the Report's recommendations are discussed with particular reference to the fragmentation of the school system and its separation from a further education market of independent colleges.

Post-war phases

Special education has been through at least three significant phases since 1944 and is now entering a fourth. The first phase, between 1944 and 1978, involved the implementation of the 1944 Education Act. It started with 11+ selection and categories of handicap and ended with comprehensive education. Between 1978 and 1986, the Warnock Report was influencing special education, while different, and not always compatible, government policies for mainstream primary and secondary education were being pursued separately. Between 1986 and 1993 providers of special education had to try to come to terms with the major changes in educational administration which, until the EA 1993, took little account of special education problems.

The first phase was based on psychological certainties. Special education was distinguished from remedial education. The former was seen as providing for categories of life-long handicaps for which there were appropriate special curricula. Remedial education, on the other hand, assumed that literacy and learning difficulties in primary and secondary schools could be solved by short-term intervention. Children with severe and profound learning difficulties were deemed ineducable.

During the 1960s and 1970s, the adverse effects of selection, testing and categorization were recognized, as comprehensive education was introduced. As part of this trend, the Education (Handicapped Children) Act 1970 abolished the category 'ineducable' and made education available to all children. The developments which followed were one of the outstanding features of special education during the last half of this phase (Tomlinson 1982; Gulliford, 1989; Adams 1990).

In the second phase following the Warnock Report, special education moved (albeit slowly and hesitantly) from a bipartite system of special schools and remedial services, towards an integrated and comprehensive special education service. The Report introduced the concept of a continuum of individual special educational needs to be met by a range of provision and services planned by local education authorities. During this period, major developments took place in the work of special schools and support services for primary and secondary schools. Primary and secondary schools were expected to take increasing responsibility for meeting special educational needs.

Starting in the 1980s, the government became concerned about general educational standards and began reforming the school and college system. This third phase involved much new legislation and regulation. A National Curriculum was introduced, the powers of LEAs were reduced and more responsibility for management and finance was given to individual schools. During this major reorganization, little direct thought was given to the management of special education and the responsibilities of primary and secondary schools for meeting special educational needs. The theory and practice of special education was not seriously considered when creating a market-oriented education system.

The concept of education

Some of the implications of the Education (Handicapped Children) Act 1970 (DES 1970) have still not been widely appreciated. The Act was passed on the basis of making education available to all children however profoundly and severely disabled. In the comprehensive and inclusive educational climate of the time, this was a proposition to which few objected. However, it soon became apparent that the traditional concept of '3 Rs' education was being challenged by the educational needs of those with severe learning difficulties. In fact, the Act implicitly broadened the definition of education. Instead of being something which was based primarily on the acquisition of literacy and numeracy skills, the definition was widened to include any planned programme delivered by educators, for enhancing personal growth and social competence (see, for example, the Newsom Report – *Half Our Future* (DES 1963) and the Plowden Report – *Children and their Primary Schools* (DES 1967)). The severe learning difficulty sector of special education led the way in special education curriculum development. During the 1970s all schools, including special schools, were responsible for their own curricula. Within a context of examination requirements, advice from the then Schools Council and from LEA advisers, schools had considerable freedom to devise and deliver the curricula they considered appropriate for their pupils. Special schools were no different in this respect, and their curricula were part of the general range on offer in LEA schools.

The introduction of a national curriculum was in some senses a return to a '3 Rs' concept of education. The insistence on a core of 'academic subjects' and a reduced emphasis on education for personal and social skills had at least two main effects in special education. It challenged existing curricula, which was no bad thing, but at the same time it reduced the time available for important aspects of special education such as the development of personal and social skills.

The introduction of national testing with the National Curriculum stressed the weaknesses rather than the strengths of those with special educational needs. The introduction of levels of attainment and national testing based on four key stages has resulted in children with special educational needs being judged against criteria formulated for children of *average* ability. There is now a real need to re-examine the objectives of special education in the context of current national educational objectives.

The separation of further education from education in schools and from adult education also modified the concept of post-school education. Government policies decreed that further education should lead to vocational proficiency and adult education be confined to education for leisure, in spite of traditions to the contrary. As will be seen in Chapter 7, the vocational slant to further education and its separation from the school system has resulted in additional problems for young people with disabilities and learning difficulties seeking post-school education and training.

The Warnock Report

The Warnock Report (DES 1978) had a major impact on the development of special education. It recommended the abolition of categories of handicap and proposed that the definition of special educational needs should include both children previously described as handicapped and those with learning difficulties of all kinds previously receiving remedial education. The Committee proposed that LEAs should plan a range of special educational provision for a range of special educational needs. It's three priority areas for action were provision for children under five, special education teacher education, and post-school provision in further and adult education.

The Report recommended that children with severe, complex and long-term needs should have a record of their needs to safeguard their provision. A number of other recommendations covered support services for schools, assessment, and inter-agency cooperation. The Report also paid considerable attention to the needs of parents.

When published in 1978, the Report was well received by almost all concerned with education and its general philosophy was endorsed. Many LEAs began reviewing their services and introducing new procedures based on the Report's recommendations. However, a change of government slowed down the consultation process and delayed action on its proposals. It was not until 1981 that an Education Act based on some of the Report's recommendations was passed, and, by that time, government education policies were becoming more market oriented.

Integration

The integration of pupils with special educational needs into the regular education system was an important issue in all developed countries from the middle of this century. Experience in the United States and Scandinavia, together with the development of comprehensive education, made it a talking point throughout the 1970s (OECD/CERI 1981, 1985). The provision of special education in mainstream primary and secondary schools was encouraged by the Warnock Report, although it was very guarded about the abolition of separate provision in special schools.

At the time, there were two main sources of pressure, both for and against integration: LEA policies and parental choice. A number of LEAs were strongly pro-integration but others were opposed to it. Parental opinions were divided with strong lobbies for both integration and the retention of special schools. Definitions of integration, which varied from simple presence in the same class or school to shared educational activities, were related to a comprehensive primary and secondary school system. In many cases the issue was side-stepped by making integrated provision and support for individuals in primary and secondary schools available, as well as continuing to fund existing special school provision. The increased recognition of parental choice resulted in limited resources being spent on both separate and integrated provision.

The theme remains an important one for special education, although the changes in the primary and secondary school system have altered its emphasis. Instead of entry to a common system of schools available to all, it has become a question of access to the same range of schools as other children of the same age. Integration will be discussed more fully in the context of the 1990s legislation in Chapter 9.

The 1981 Education Act

This Act implemented those parts of the Warnock Report that the government thought might cost nothing. It introduced new relative definitions of special educational needs and provision. It established a new system of statutory assessment and statements of needs and provision for pupils with severe, complex and long-term needs. The LEA was made responsible for securing the provision set out in statements. The Act also specified conditions for providing integrated provision.

Although the 1981 Act created the conditions for pre-school provision, little action followed. Provision post-school was left for later consideration. The Warnock Report's teacher training priority was ignored, but after a time, funds were made available for the training of teachers in primary and secondary schools to become SEN coordinators (Cowne and Norwich 1987; Moses and Hegarty 1988). Following the passing of the Act, the DES appeared to concentrate solely on issues relating to children who were the subject of statements.

However, many LEAs, schools and colleges of further education began to take steps to implement the Warnock Report more fully. Links between special schools and primary and secondary schools increased (Jowett *et al.* 1988), support teaching services were developed (Moses *et al.* 1988) and the range of post-school provision increased (Stowell 1987). This progress was maintained until the late 1980s.

Research

The DES funded a research programme to monitor the effects of the 1981 Act on policy and provision for special educational needs. Research projects were carried out by the National Foundation for Educational Research (NFER), the University of London Institute of Education (ULIE) and a team from Manchester University and Huddersfield Polytechnic. The aspects of special education covered were: the implementation of the 1981 Act by LEAs (the ULIE project); provision for SEN in primary and secondary schools (the NFER project); and in-service training programmes for special educational needs teachers (the Manchester/Huddersfield project). The findings from the three projects have been published in: Goacher *et al.* 1988; Jowett *et al.* 1988; Moses *et al.* 1988; Robson *et al.* 1988; Evans *et al.* 1989.

Key findings from the ULIE project on the impact of the 1981 Act in LEAs were that:

- there was some confusion about the term 'special educational needs' and its use in practice;
- the statutory assessment procedures were perceived as problematic and time consuming;
- the notion of parental partnership had yet to become a reality;
- a shortage of resources was hindering the full implementation of the Act;
- inter-agency communication and collaboration were causing difficulties;
- planning and policy-making for SEN were not coherent or consistent.

The government responded to problems with the assessment procedures by issuing Circular 22/89 (DES 1989) and its Addendum, but further developments in policy for special education at the national level were superseded by the introduction of the National Curriculum and LMS.

Developments in the 1980s

As the decade developed, more and more government attention was paid to educational standards in primary and secondary education. Socialist LEA policies, and to some extent comprehensive schools, were blamed for low standards (CCCS 1981; Ball 1990). Attention moved from individual to national needs and from school systems to individual schools. The results have already been described.

From the special education point of view, a philosophical difference emerged between the search for national standards based on national testing which would grade children's level of achievements and the individual and relative approach to learning difficulties evident in the 1981 Act (Russell 1990; Wedell 1990). The responsibilities of primary and secondary schools for meeting special educational needs were not apparently considered or defined at the time.

Responsibilities for further education were taken away from LEAs and given to a new national quango, the Further Education Funding Council (FEFC). Colleges subsequently became free-standing individual institutions under the FHEA 1992.

Although extra funds were made available to education, they were mainly used to introduce and publicize new management arrangements and curricula. Most of the resources now available to LEAs had to be distributed to individual schools. Limited funds for special education were distributed more widely in smaller amounts with few controls on their use. There was little guidance about the use of the notional percentages, in block grants, for meeting the special educational needs of children without statements. The use of available funds was not monitored and little evidence was obtained about their effective use.

This then was the situation at the beginning of the 1990s. Subsequent chapters concentrate on the present and future. Before doing so, it may be helpful to look at the nature of special educational needs, an issue central to their management in the education system. Definitions are discussed at this point as an introduction to the consideration of the outcomes of 1990s legislation.

Special needs and special educational needs

These terms have been used by many as inter-changeable and as synonyms. The use of the two terms loosely leads to problems. In practice schools are expected to meet a variety of *special needs* but are only legally required to meet *special educational needs*. Because special educational needs are defined in law in the EA 1993, it is important to distinguish them from the other special needs with which schools are faced.

In the discussion which follows, the term *special needs* will refer only to the broader group of needs. This includes children who are gifted, belong to another culture, have a mother tongue other than English, or are members of travelling and Gypsy families or service families. In addition, children in the care of local authorities may have special needs as may children living in adverse social and economic circumstances. Only some of the children in these groups may have *special educational needs*, but all may require some additional attention and resources if they are to benefit fully from their education.

There has been criticism of the concept of special educational needs because of the variety of other special needs evident in schools. In addition to effective class and subject teaching, there are only a limited number of ways in which schools can meet special needs of all kinds. Indeed, it is not practicable for many schools to provide differentiated programmes for each special need. It is often difficult for schools to provide separate programmes for giftedness and English as a second language.

To distinguish programmes for disruptive pupils from those for pupils whose behaviour difficulties are deemed to be special educational needs is virtually impossible.

The statutory requirement to provide for special educational needs may distort a school's response to the range of special needs in its pupils. Giftedness is the only special need viewed positively by educators, and parental choice and school differentiation will meet the needs of most children who are gifted, although a small minority may require special provision. Schools need incentives and additional resources to meet other needs. In the long run the use of the term *special educational needs* at school level may prove unhelpful and a broad concept of special need for learning support may more properly describe what is required.

A good case could be made for a single element in school budgets designed to provide for a range of special needs which cause children to require learning support. Such an element should be based on an agreed formula taking into account variations in school populations and the catchment areas from which they admit pupils (for example, the Nottinghamshire LMS scheme). The school audit approach developed by some authorities (for example, Kent) for special educational needs could be extended to include the whole range of special needs.

The nature of special educational needs

Because of the variety of special needs arising in schools, it is important to be clear about the nature of special educational needs, which are defined in the 1981 and 1993 Education Acts as significant learning difficulties or as impediments to the use of the same educational facilities as others. The definitions in the Acts replaced categories of handicap which had been in existence since 1944. The 1981 Act definitions were derived from the recommendations of the Warnock Report. The Report did not subscribe to the individual deficit approach to special education, but envisaged a range of special educational needs arising from disabilities and learning difficulties.

These needs, it was thought, arose from a combination of factors including individual characteristics, individual experiences, home circumstances and school environments. However, the tradition of categories of handicap based on a diagnosis of an individual's disabilities, remains a potent influence on thinking. Administrators need terms to describe the pupils admitted to different kinds of special school and other forms of provision. Those working in special education wish to describe the problems of the children with whom they work. As a result a form of categorization continues to exist (Norwich 1990).

The move away from an individual deficit model of special education was also retarded by the introduction of procedures for making statements of individual needs and provision introduced by the 1981 Act. Statements were for children whose disabilities and difficulties were severe, long term and complex. These procedures tended to focus on the functioning of individual children.

Definitions

Definitions of needs and criteria for statements were both major sources of concern in the 1980s and there are continuing problems with definitions. Three different areas of definition lead to disagreement and uncertainty:

- descriptions of disabilities and learning difficulties;
- descriptions of the educational and other needs which may arise from them;
- descriptions of the nature of provision to be made for the established needs.

Disabilities and difficulties

Defining different kinds and degrees of disability or learning difficulty is easier than defining the special educational needs which may arise from them. Physical and sensory disabilities may be amenable to precise medical description as may some forms of severe intellectual disability and psychiatric illness. In the case of marked disabilities and difficulties, social and family circumstances may have less influence on the special educational needs which may arise.

Areas of cognitive disfunction and behavioural difficulty are often less amenable to precise description. Many of the common learning and behaviour difficulties are found, in practice, to be associated with either minor physical and sensory disabilities and/or social and family conditions which may interfere with learning.

In all instances, a child's personality and response will influence the extent to which a disability or difficulty may affect his or her educational progress. Thus the degree to which a disability or difficulty may give rise to a special educational need will depend on individual circumstances. Even where it is possible to be precise about a degree of disability, it is not possible to be equally precise about the needs which may arise or the provision needed.

For example, a hearing disability may be defined by decibel loss with some accuracy but its consequence for the individual will depend on a number of factors. These include the individual's intelligence and family circumstances and the educational context in which he or she is placed. The learning difficulty which arises has to be assessed not only in terms of hearing loss but also in terms of language development and educational progress. A relative judgement will be made on a range of evidence. Similarly, appropriate provision will be a matter of parental choice and professional judgement.

Definitions of special educational needs

The legal definition of special educational needs is a relative one based on the performance of a child's contemporaries. Relativity poses practical problems at the school level and LEA level. Each individual school is expected to make a judgement about the existence of a significant learning difficulty relative to other pupils not only in the school but also in the area. Each LEA has to decide whether a child's learning difficulty is significant, whether the child should be formally assessed and whether, as a result of that assessment, the child should become the subject of a statement of needs and provision.

The new Code of Practice sets out five stages of assessment similar to those suggested in the Warnock Report. Schools, from small village primary schools to large urban secondary schools, are expected to carry out the first three stages before referral to LEAs. At the third stage, schools should make use of external psychological and support teaching services. Although the Code sets out standard procedures in detail, criteria for the existence of special educational needs are expressed in very general terms. It is argued that the current concentration on diagnosis and individual learning programmes in the Code of Practice places too much emphasis on personal deficits and too little on deficiencies in teaching and school provision.

The assessment of individual progress on the National Curriculum has been treated quite separately from the assessment of special educational needs. Initially such testing was also assumed to have a diagnostic purpose, but this aspect of the assessment was subsequently abandoned. Standardized tests and the ranking of pupils and schools on the basis of such test results are the means by which national standards and progress in the National Curriculum are assessed. The DFE approach takes little account of regional, local and school differences.

Procedures for the assessment of special educational needs have continued to be treated separately from national curriculum assessment in Circulars of Guidance. Schools are now expected to carry out two different procedures to record pupil progress, which have much in common but which have inconsistent objectives.

Assessment procedures have become increasingly refined in recent years and it is now possible to list many different syndromes from which needs arise. However, there remains uncertainty and a lack of clarity about the relative contributions of physical and psychological factors and of social and environmental factors in the genesis of special educational needs. Many issues about the assessment of special educational needs have to be addressed if schools and parents are to be satisfied that procedures have improved.

As already noted, the LEA is required to decide whether to accept that a child referred by a school has a special educational need, whether to carry out a statutory assessment and whether to make a statement. Although an LEA can collect information from the schools in its area, it may be difficult for it to gather consistent information about standards on which to base decisions. National criteria and consistent standards are expected by parents and politicians, but the means of achieving them are far from clear.

Defining special educational provision

Defining the nature of provision also presents difficulties for schools and LEAs. In the period after the 1944 Education Act, it was assumed that children could be categorized and that for each category there would be appropriate curricula and pedagogy. Later it was realized that many children with special educational needs have a number of disabilities and do not fall neatly into categories.

As most provision at the time was made in separate special schools, and subsequently in separate special classes, a second definition based on location came into use. Special education was what happened in special schools and classes. A third kind of definition arose from the activities of teachers with experience and/or training in special education. Provision was defined in terms of their work (Fish 1989). The legal definition of provision is broad and simply refers to arrangements that are different from or additional to provision made for children of the same age.

The government, in the guise of the DFE, has never defined provision in any more detail. Very little guidance has been given about what should be available. While the resource implications of being specific may have inhibited giving guidance, the fact remains that there is little to help those responsible for making provision to decide what is or is not acceptable as special education.

Thus there are continuing issues about forms of provision. Many definitions of provision exist, some promoted by special interests. Parents, voluntary organizations and LEAs are often at variance about the nature of what should be provided for particular learning difficulties. But the new Code and regulations do nothing to develop a standard or national definition of provision, or to indicate the nature of the provision which parents might reasonably expect to be available. The government has issued various Charters for users of public services, including one for parents (DFE 1994a) and one for parents of children with special educational needs (DFE 1994b). However, these Charters are mainly concerned with process issues and do not lay down in any detail what provision schools can be expected to make.

The nature of special education

The new Code of Practice recognizes that a range of provision should be available to meet a range of needs. Although special educational needs are comparatively easy to define, the parameters of provision to meet them has received far less attention. The EA 1993 states that special educational provision is that which is additional to or different from provision made for other children of the same age in the area.

Although parents now expect the same range and quality of provision wherever they live, and although the DFE recognizes the importance of national standards, other policies are making it more difficult to ensure that a range of provision is available. As purchasers rather than providers, LEAs have fewer powers and resources to develop provision. Primary, secondary and special schools are now relatively independent providers and, furthermore, the FAS has powers to set up grant-maintained special schools.

It is now possible to choose from a range of individual learning programmes said to meet defined needs. However, data on the effectiveness of different forms of provision is limited. In practice, there is a difference between the detailed specification of provision, which is expected in statements, and the very general descriptions of provision for other pupils with special educational needs. Although the special educational provision made by primary and secondary schools now has to be specified in school policy statements, there are no guidelines about what they might be expected to provide.

The characteristics of provision

The words to describe needs and provision may change with time and fashion but the parameters of special educational provision do not change. An attempt to define those parameters was made in *What is Special Education?* (Fish 1989). Some 16 characteristics were identified of which perhaps the following are the most important – time, expertise, technology, environments and relationships. All have resource implications.

The one common feature in meeting special educational needs is the need for **time** to give the individual or group more attention, more support and more teaching. This time may be given by non-teaching assistants, by regular teachers and by special education teachers, but to be effective its use needs to be planned and supervised by a trained special education teacher.

The special education teacher must bring **expertise** to bear on the identified needs, either directly or through the actions of regular teachers or non-teaching assistants. Although it has been the practice to have specially trained teachers to work with children with hearing and visual difficulties, it has never been possible to ensure that all teachers with special education responsibilities have had appropriate additional training. Thus the levels of expertise of designated special education teachers may vary widely.

Technology is making an increasing contribution to the field. Starting from the early days of low vision aids, hearing aids and induction loops, micro-technology and information technology have been making an increasing contribution. Technology enables many more children to have access to the national curriculum and to manage their own learning. It also enables some children to be less dependent on special environments (Vincent 1989).

Special **environments** have always played a part in provision. The most obvious are the acoustic environments to enhance aural perception. But they are equally important for children with some physical disabilities and for some emotional and behaviour difficulties.

While all effective special education is dependent on good **relationships**, it is in the area of emotional and behaviour difficulties that they may be crucial. This parameter is more especially related to the quality of provision rather than to its extent.

Conclusion

The recent history of special education has been one of expansion and development. A more general acceptance of the existence of needs has not been accompanied by clarity about their nature. *Special needs* and *special educational needs* are confused. As a subgroup of the harder to teach and slower to learn, pupils with *special educational needs* are receiving particular attention perhaps to the detriment of other special needs. The next chapter will take the discussion of provision further in the context of mainstream primary and secondary schools.

5 / Meeting Needs in Schools

Meeting needs starts in pre-school provision and continues up to the age of 16 or 18+. Early intervention programmes and close contacts between nursery, primary, secondary and special education are important if children and young people with disabilities and learning difficulties are to have ready access to the same range of opportunities as others. This chapter will look at the interface between mainstream and special education during the school period and the implications of new legislation for their close association. Other themes to be discussed include the nature of provision in schools, the responsibilities of governors, senior managers and special educational needs (SEN) coordinators and the preparation and training required fully to implement the EA 1993.

Provision for under fives

Provision for children under five with special educational needs was limited and patchy before the Warnock Committee made it a priority area for development. The Committee's recommendations have never been fully implemented. After the Report, there was a significant increase in attention to the special educational needs of children in existing playgroups, nurseries and nursery schools, but little additional nursery or other provision was made. A number of different models of provision were identified. Opportunity Groups were one example of part-time pre-school facilities. Children with and without disabilities experienced nursery education together. Those with disabilities also received therapies and special teaching, while their parents received support from meeting as a group. Integrated nurseries, where young children with and without special educational needs learned together, were developed by some LEAs. An important new initiative was the introduction of Portage-type schemes. The Portage approach and material were developed in the USA and consist of a multi-professional management committee supervising a group of professionals from a wide range of disciplines who are trained to work with parents. They introduce and support systematic home teaching programmes which are developed from the Portage materials (Portage Project 1976).

The materials cover all aspects of early child development and consist of defined behaviours and skills to be taught by parents. The Portage workers help parents to choose the behaviours and skills they wish to develop with their children and support them as they carry out an agreed programme. After pilot projects, the scheme was successfully introduced to the United Kingdom (Cameron 1986). The Portage project was one of a number of initiatives in the USA designed to reduce the effects of disabilities, early social deprivation and subsequent school failure. Although there remains disagreement about the outcomes of these programmes (Warfield 1994), the importance of pre-school programmes in improving the educational response of the harder to educate has been officially recognized in the USA. Although it acknowledges the value of pre-school education, the DFE has no policy for its development.

If parents do not choose or are unable to take part in home-based teaching programmes, there are alternatives. The range of possible provision includes child minding, pre-school play groups, nurseries, nursery classes and nursery schools with social services responsible for all except nursery classes and schools. Although there has been increasing support for nursery education for all children, there has generally been a lack of resources and a lack of will to make provision (National Commission on Education 1993). A lack of resources for local authority under-five services prevents sufficient provision being made and in practice limits agency contributions to joint provision. Provision during this period requires close cooperation between education, health and social services but this has proved hard to develop in an era of changing policies and limited resources (Goacher *et al.* 1988).

The new Code of Practice devotes a separate section to children with special educational needs under five, placing responsibilities on all services and providers to initiate action and inform parents. The wishes of parents and the support they need are central to the Code's approach.

The Code clarifies intentions but leaves many practical difficulties unresolved. Much depends on parental initiative. If parents choose not to take action when informed of their children's needs, there is little that many agencies can do. If facilities and agencies are not well informed about special educational needs and of the importance of early intervention, they are unlikely to be active in persuading parents to take action.

The delegation of management responsibilities to primary schools appears to have led to more provision being made for four-year-olds and may lead to more nursery class provision for parents able to pay for it. Special provision may also be developed by special schools. But it is likely that pre-school choices will remain limited for those parents whose children have significant special educational needs.

Although the value of early childhood programmes of all kinds has been demonstrated – particularly in raising school standards and reducing later social and educational problems – there are no signs that provision is being given any national priority. The short-term saving of resources in the pre-school years is apparently considered more important than possible long-term savings in educational costs throughout a child's school life.

Provision in schools

The response of schools to the learning and behaviour difficulties of the pupils who attend them is the key to appropriate provision to meet special educational needs. Because schools can create as well as meet such needs, their response to them is closely linked to the effective management of learning. When dealing with many of the common learning and behaviour difficulties, the differences between good teaching and special education teaching are hard to detect (Ainscow 1991). Schools now have a clear responsibility to meet special educational needs in their pupils. The EA 1993 and the Code set out general guidelines but there remain many unresolved difficulties for schools. The relationship between special needs and special educational needs was discussed in the previous chapter. Other challenges for schools are discussed in the following sections.

The background

Forms of provision

There are a limited number of ways in which schools have made provision for special needs. It may be helpful to describe them briefly as a background to defining special educational provision. Provision in primary and secondary schools may include:

- forms of team teaching which include meeting special needs;
- providing extra teaching support in the regular classroom;
- providing extra non-teaching support in the regular classroom;
- withdrawal from regular classes for periods of extra tuition either individually or in small groups;
- giving additional tuition in breaks during the school day;
- providing full or part-time special education in separate units within the school.

The Code of Practice now stipulates that pupils with special educational needs involved in these approaches will have an appropriate individual education plan (IEP).

Team teaching

Where two or more teachers work together as a team responsible for a group of pupils, it becomes possible for one of the team to spend time with small groups with special needs. These needs may include giftedness, English as a second language, or having special educational needs. This type of provision can be helpful with children with the less severe learning and behaviour difficulties.

Teaching support in the classroom

Support teaching occurs when another teacher spends periods in primary or secondary school classes helping children with special needs. The additional teacher helps the children concerned to complete assignments agreed with the class or subject teacher. When effective, and when the additional teacher has special education skills, this is another form of team teaching. However, there is seldom sufficient time to provide the support teaching which pupils need and such provision is usually only available in a minority of lessons. Nor is there sufficient time for class or subject teachers to work with the support teacher to plan appropriate assignments. There is some evidence of the effectiveness of in-class support but little information about the minimum support time necessary to meet particular needs. Although an attractive approach, it is rarely adequately staffed or comprehensively carried out.

Non-teaching support in the classroom

The provision of non-teaching help to class teachers is common in nursery and infant schools, and, in the primary phase, can be part of normal staffing. Tight budgets are causing primary school managers to make a choice between appointing qualified teachers and non-teaching assistants (NTAs). Recent research (Evans *et al.* 1994a, 1994b) has indicated that schools are increasingly choosing to employ NTAs in preference to qualified teachers.

More recently, the provision of NTAs has become an important element in meeting special educational needs in primary and secondary schools. Either as a result of an assessment of non-statement needs, or as part of an individual's statement provision, schools may be given a number of additional NTAs. Assistance can take two main forms: personal assistance to enable children to carry out classroom activities; and assistance with school work under the supervision of the teacher concerned. The value of such assistance is recognized but its effectiveness has not been evaluated in any detail. Preparation and training for teachers and assistants to work together varies widely.

Withdrawal

Provision of this kind involves a teacher with special education responsibilities withdrawing individuals or small groups from a number of lessons for special teaching. These arrangements are most commonly made for pupils with reading difficulties but are also made for some pupils with hearing impairments or behaviour difficulties.

Additional tuition

The only difference from withdrawal is that special help is provided outside normally timetabled hours.

Full or part-time units

Special education units may be set up by schools but are more commonly set up with LEA support. Part-time units are usually associated with supported periods in a child's own class. Full-time units are for short-term intensive programmes or are planned for the purposes of social interaction rather than shared education. Units normally provide for a single disability, such as visual or hearing impairment, or a particular group of learning and behavioural needs. The extent to which different forms of provision can be made is influenced by the size and nature of schools. In primary schools, support teaching and withdrawal are the most common approaches. Units in primary schools are usually financed by LEAs and cater for children who are the subject of statements. Provision at secondary level is usually closely related to school organization and the grouping of pupils. Most forms of provision can be found at secondary level, including units for pupils who are the subject of statements, also financed by LEAs. School provision of all kinds may or may not be supplemented by support teaching services. Because of the variety of arrangements, the effectiveness of different approaches is uncertain.

In the 'remedial education' era, (1960s and 1970s), research showed that short-term gains were not sustained in the long term (Collins 1961). More recently, Reading Recovery Programmes have shown remarkable gains in proficiency over three to four months but the long-term effects of such programmes are not yet known (Wright 1992; Hall 1994; Wright 1994).

Primary and secondary teaching

Whatever the form of provision adopted by a school, the class or form teacher will be expected to make a major contribution to meeting special educational needs. Limited resources for support-teaching services mean that they are more likely to receive advice than regular practical help. But class and subject teachers are faced nowadays with children who are unsettled for a variety of reasons, such as divorce, refugee status, poverty, homelessness and many other special needs.

The Primary Class Teacher has a wide range of responsibilities. These include preparing and teaching the National Curriculum, keeping a detailed teaching record, maintaining detailed records of individual pupil progress and writing regular reports for parents. The unsettled background of many primary-age children is an important factor in making teaching more difficult and stressful. This additional burden must be recognized when considering how much a class teacher can contribute to meeting a range of special needs, including special educational needs. In addition to perhaps five or six children with special educational needs, the primary class teacher may expect to find a significant proportion of children whose approach to learning may be temporarily affected by family circumstances. There will be those whose parent's marriages are breaking up or who are having to adjust to new parental partnerships. There will also be a number of children whose social circumstances influence their behaviour and ability to learn. In some areas there will be children from transient families and with different cultural backgrounds. In addition, there may also be children whose special needs arise from unusually high ability in one or more areas of the curriculum.

All these special needs make demands on planning and teaching time additional to those made by the Code to assess, report on and plan programmes for pupils identified as having special educational needs. It is against this background that it is necessary to consider whether the new legislation is realistic and its implementation in primary schools a practical possibility.

Secondary Phase pupils will have the same unsettled backgrounds as primary children with the additional tensions which may arise as they grow through adolescence. Drink, drugs and sexual relationships may all intrude into their social lives and influence motivation and learning. Both form tutors and subject teachers will be faced with the effects of these pressures on learning.

Subject specialist teachers may, in practice, teach 150–200 different pupils each week, and at the same time they are expected to keep a detailed record of each pupil's progress. In recent years the introduction, alteration and testing of the National Curriculum have been major burdens. In addition to the unsettled states of many of their pupils, teachers will be expected to deal with all the special needs, including special educational needs, which should be met. These may be more concentrated in some teaching groups than others depending on the school's organization of teaching groups.

It is in these circumstances that all teachers are expected to contribute to the identification of special educational needs and to meeting them. What practical support are they being offered?

The nature of provision in primary and secondary schools

In practice there are three elements which might be considered to constitute special education in mainstream primary and secondary schools: the provision of special education advice and support to regular teachers; the development of individual special education programmes; and the direct teaching of children with special educational needs.

Special educational advice and support

Advice and support for class and subject teachers comes from two main sources – from special educational needs teachers on the staff of schools and from advisory and support services. In the period after the Warnock Report, an increasing number of teachers were trained to become special educational needs teachers in schools and most large primary schools and secondary schools now have such a teacher. They are able to identify, assess and meet the more common special educational needs.

At the same time, advisory and support services were reorganized and increased in size. The development of advisory and support services changed the activities of many special education teachers. From working directly with small groups of pupils, for example with reading difficulties, withdrawn from their classes, they changed to advising class teachers and helping them to prepare and manage individual learning programmes. Providing support to class and subject teachers was seen as one of the best means of meeting the wider range of needs in primary and secondary schools. The allocation of time from such services was also an element in provision for individuals with statements. The existence of such services can be said to be a form of provision. But, unless children can be assured of either regular teaching from a member of a service or regular planned oversight of their individual programme, one would question whether *special education* was being provided. The work of these services will be discussed more fully in the next chapter.

The development of individual programmes

An individual education programme (IEP), devised as the result of assessment, is seen as an important element in all forms of special education. Indeed, it is the main form of provision in primary and secondary schools specified in the Code of Practice. At the same time, the effective teaching of class groups involves the management of learning which in turn involves planning appropriate individual learning programmes. Thus individual programmes may be part of both regular and special education. It is easy to identify special education programmes where there are marked differences from those used in regular education, for example, a programme for a blind pupil using braille and audio texts. For physical and sensory disabilities, individual programmes may be distinguished by special materials and methods. But differences become much less clear when considering programmes for pupils with learning and behaviour difficulties. The less marked the disability, the fewer special materials and methods are necessary and hence the nearer they become to individual programmes in regular education (Wedell 1995).

Managing a range of rates and styles of learning in a regular class, and planning work accordingly may involve personal programmes which recognize individual differences, whereas *special education* programmes may be concerned with specific approaches and techniques to meet identified learning difficulties. What distinguishes good education from *special education* is not simply an academic question. Schools and LEAs will not only have to decide whether a pupil has or has not special educational needs but also whether an individual education programme is a *special education* one.

Special education teaching

The most obvious form of provision is to be taught by staff with appropriate training and experience in special education. One result of policies of integration has been to reduce separate special teaching and to replace it with specialist and non-teaching support for class and subject teachers. An issue, in primary and secondary schools is the extent to which pupils with identified special educational needs should have regular direct or indirect contact with a specialist teacher before provision can be said to be made.

Responsibilities

One of the major changes introduced by the EA 1993 and the Code of Practice is the specification of the responsibilities of primary and secondary schools for special education. This became necessary when schools were given a form of independence and LEAs were expected to service rather than manage a local school system. The Code of Practice sets out detailed guidance. This includes recommended procedures which schools must follow 'in spirit' if not in precise detail. The foreword to the Code states that schools must have regard to the Code but each must decide how to fulfil their duties. This is one of the consequences of applying the same responsibilities and procedures to all schools ranging in size from small, rural primary schools to large, urban secondary schools.

Governors and headteachers

The duties of governors to secure necessary provision to meet special educational needs and other related matters are now clearly defined in law. Together with the headteacher, they are expected to determine a school's general policy and approach to special educational needs and maintain an oversight of its implementation. The headteacher is responsible for implementing the school's special educational policy, and for ensuring the quality of the provision made, as part of the management of all aspects of a school's work.

The SEN coordinator

Schools are expected to have a special educational needs coordinator. He or she is expected to be responsible for:

- the day-to-day operation of the school's SEN policy;
- liaising with and advising fellow teachers;
- planning and coordinating provision for children with SEN;
- maintaining the school's register of and records on pupils with SEN;
- liaising with their parents and external agencies and services;
- contributing to in-service training.

The SEN coordinator is seen as having a vital role in ensuring that the school-based stages of assessment and provision are carried out and in preparing reports for LEAs when further action is thought necessary. It is envisaged that the SEN coordinator should make two main contributions in the school: first, as a manager of assessment procedures and provision; and second, as the school's specialist for special educational needs. In small schools, the coordinator may be the head or deputy, and in large schools there may be a team of teachers fulfilling this role. Where heads and deputies are concerned, they may make an effective management contribution but not necessarily a specialist one. The reverse may be true when teachers are appointed for their specialist skills but are given little time or status to manage provision. The time taken for the SEN coordinator to implement the Code effectively in schools of different sizes and populations has not apparently been estimated and thus the resource implications of the Code are not defined (Bibby 1994).

Class and subject teachers

The Code places considerable emphasis on individual education programmes to which class and subject teachers are expected to make a major contribution. Their responsibilities for meeting special educational needs are assumed, with little account taken of the time and effort necessary. There is apparently little recognition of the effect of the changes which have resulted in many special education teachers moving from the direct provision of special education to the indirect support of classroom teacher managed programmes.

Currently, attention is often centred on the nature of programmes. Responsibility for the nature and effectiveness of special education programmes is far from clear when the level of expertise within individual schools cannot be assured. This is an issue which will have to be resolved.

Support services

Responsibilities for the nature and quality of support services have not been resolved by the new legislation. Although it is made clear that LEAs remain responsible for the services required for statutory assessment and for implementing statements, the Code is not clear about other services for schools. As the House of Commons report (HOC 1993) states:

> The extent to which primary and secondary schools can make effective provision for a range of special educational needs depends not only on the skills of the school staff but also on the contribution of a variety of psychological and support teaching services . . . the future contribution of these services to provision is apparently to depend on whether schools will pay for them. If support services are no longer free at the point of delivery, and schools have to pay for them, they might choose not to pay for them.
>
> (HOC 1993: vol. 1, p. xvi)

The Report goes on to recommend that school policy statements should include the use they intend to make of support services and that such services should be required to register their qualifications. It was also recommended that the DFE should issue guidelines about the staffing and functions of services and how they should be managed and financed. Of all these proposals, only the first was implemented and the Code requires school policy statements to specify the support services they use. But as the Committee's Report states 'The future role of support services is ill defined' (ibid.).

Issues for schools

The special education issues for schools follow a sequence from policy to practice. Policies will be determined, in part, by funding priorities and the Code. It will be some time before the relative influences of the FAS and LEAs are clear. Because LEAs retain responsibility for pupils with statements, grant-maintained school policies will be influenced by both FAS and LEA policies, whereas LEA-maintained schools will only be influenced by LEA policies.

School policies and special education

The policy and priorities for a school as a whole will influence its special education policy. For example its approach to the education of below-average pupils will be crucial. Whatever the organization adopted by the school, the quality and quantity of the resources devoted to the less successful pupils will be significant. The policy may or may not recognize the part played by the school's organization and methods in creating special educational needs. It can also treat those needs as transitory or long term. But, more importantly, it will define the priority given to meeting special educational needs, expressed in terms of resources (time, expertise, facilities and money).

School special education policies

The Code provides detailed guidance about the form of the policy statement. While it specifies assessment procedures in detail, guidance about provision is very general. Pupils identified as having special educational needs should have an individual education plan. Schools are expected to use unspecified advisory and support services. As indicated earlier, schools are expected to determine the provision they can make, but they are not required to ensure that any particular form or level of provision is available. The availability and quality of provision will be monitored by parents' response to annual school reports and by four-yearly inspections.

Provision

The greatest problem for schools will be to determine priorities in the use of limited resources. If the notional percentage for meeting needs delegated to schools via the formula is made available for provision by the school, it is still unlikely to be sufficient to meet all special needs. It will be necessary to determine what forms of provision are possible, appropriate and practicable. The Code also requires considerable time to be devoted to assessment and report writing. As with much development since the Warnock Report, it is possible that more resources will be devoted to identifying and assessing needs than to meeting them. What should be the priorities of an SEN coordinator and what contribution to provision can be expected when, for example, in a small primary school only one session a fortnight is made available to the coordinator?

Schools and LEAs

The Code recommends that, after the first three stages of provision have proved inappropriate or ineffective, schools should approach LEAs to request statutory assessment with a view to making a statement. It is at this point that two difficulties may arise in practice. Without detailed knowledge of school standards and practices, LEAs will find it hard to determine levels of learning difficulty or need. A second source of difficulty is that, at this point, LEAs are also in a position to refer pupils back to schools with recommendations for further action by schools. This interface between schools and LEAs, with parents as a third party, may become a difficult division of responsibilities. Both schools and LEAs will need very clear policy statements, if disagreements and appeals are not to bedevil meeting children's needs.

Training

Although there has been a programme to train SEN coordinators for some years, the new legislation, together with the Code, comprises a complex series of changes for which governors, senior staff and coordinators will need further training. Above all the independence of schools and the uncertainty about support services, or the ability to pay for them, will require the further development of SEN coordinator skills. The financing of training from within school budgets will again be related to school priorities. As the Audit Commission/HMI Report (1992a) pointed out, incentives are necessary if schools are to take special educational responsibilities seriously and at present such incentives do not exist.

Evaluation

It is not easy to see how the government expects the new arrangements to be evaluated. It appears to be relying exclusively on consumer response. At present there appears to be no organization in a position to give disinterested and informed advice about effective special education to all who need it.

Conclusion

The new framework places more responsibilities on individual schools without apparently taking account of the resource and training implications of the Code or providing the means necessary to ensure that an adequate system of support services is available to them. The problems facing schools have been outlined and will be further discussed in later chapters. Whatever the policies and funding formulae devised by the DFE, the FAS and LEAs, it would be helpful if the following general principles were borne in mind. These are that:

- the better schools are resourced, the smaller the number of special educational needs which arise;
- the more effective the special educational provision made by primary and secondary schools, the smaller the number of children referred for statutory assessment;
- the more effective the psychological and special education support services available to those schools, the smaller the number of children requiring statements.

6 / A Range of Provision

There is a continuing belief, restated in the Code, that there should be a range of provision to meet a range of special educational needs. Recent legislation however, has made the development of a range more difficult because it has separated responsibility for children whose needs do not require a statement from responsibility for children who have statements. It has given both LEAs and the FAS powers to make special educational provision. Management responsibilities are now fragmented. Each individual school or college is expected to have a special education policy and to make appropriate provision to meet common but significant learning difficulties. At the same time, LEAs remain responsible for developing special education policies and practices for statutory assessment, for making statements and for securing the provision specified in them. The planning of a range of provision appears to depend on a market based on the unregulated exchange of information.

This chapter is concerned with special educational arrangements outside the responsibility of mainstream primary and secondary schools. It discusses LEAs' duties to secure provision for children who are the subject of statements in primary and secondary schools and elsewhere. It is also concerned with the development of a range of special education facilities and services within a market created by parental and student choice.

Before considering the current and future position, it may be helpful to look at two recent approaches to managing provision. One which falls between individual school arrangements and LEA provision, is the linking of schools in networks, federations and clusters. The other concerns the steps taken by LEAs to support provision in primary and secondary schools and to develop criteria for making statements.

Clusters

Various forms of collaboration between schools exist including networks, federations and clusters. Clusters came into prominence for a number of reasons including:

- to assist a group of small primary schools to share curriculum development and delivery skills;
- to enable a group of schools to share special education expertise and to adopt a common approach to meeting needs.

Through the education support grant system, the DES supported 14 LEA pilot projects concerned with collaboration between schools. They were evaluated at Leicester University (Galton *et al.* 1991) and the study identified a number of important factors in successful collaboration. More recently the DFE (DFE 1994f) has promoted clusters as a means of encouraging a group of schools to seek grant-maintained status together. This publication proposes two forms of cluster, a group of schools with a single governing board and a group of schools which delegates specific functions to a joint committee. Clusters in which schools retain their own governing bodies are not allowed to delegate their special education responsibilities.

The development of clusters for special education purposes was stimulated by the Inner London Education Authority (ILEA) Report on special education, *Education for All?* (ILEA 1985). The Fish Report, as it was called, saw clusters as enabling schools to:

- share responsibility for special educational needs;
- provide continuity in provision from phase to phase;
- create locally appropriate forms of provision;
- to provide a focus for the delivery of external services.

Around that time a number of other LEAs were encouraging similar developments. More recently a study by Lunt *et al.* (1994a) analysed the structure and working practices of a number of different arrangements. Conditions which facilitated collaboration were identified as were major factors inhibiting cooperation. Important factors included:

- the existence of a catalyst;
- the provision of recognized extra resources;
- a recognized and defined task or a particular problem to be solved;
- a level of trust between participants;
- a reward for participation;
- an acceptable coordinator.

In the current climate of change and innovation, it may be difficult for schools to appreciate the value of clusters. Pressure and financial constraints are not ideal conditions for promoting cooperation. However, as schools become more aware of their independence, the finite limits of resources and their increased responsibilities, they may look to other schools for support. Clusters may be one way to make effective use of scarce special education expertise and to enhance the provision schools are able to make.

LEA approaches to resource allocation

A number of initiatives taken by LEAs in recent years were identified by the Audit Commission (Audit Commission 1992a). The approaches of Leeds, Kent, Northamptonshire and Nottinghamshire are all instructive (HOC 1993). These initiatives attempt to assess the extent and degree of needs in individual schools and to reduce the number of pupils being made the subject of statements.

The Leeds LEA started to introduce a banding scheme in 1990–91. Just over half of the money allocated to schools for special educational needs was allocated on a free school meals formula. The remainder was allocated on the assessed needs of individual children. Children were placed in one of three bands based on the additional teacher and non-teacher time they required. The range was from a small amount of teaching or non-teaching time to a half-time teacher or a full-time non-teaching assistant. Experience resulted in the scheme being modified. Bands were discontinued and schools were allocated a number of units of resource (£500 in 1993), for identified individual children (HOC 1993: vol. II, p. 164).

Northamptonshire LEA introduced five bands in ascending order of learning difficulty. Criteria for each band were specified. Marginal problems were defined in Band 1 and mild difficulties in Band 2. It was expected that the needs of pupils in Bands 1 and 2 would be met from funds allocated to schools including additional elements based on an audit of pupil needs. Band 3 was crucial to the scheme. It was the point at which significant difficulties were defined and it was expected that schools would refer pupils for statutory assessment. Bands 4 and 5 defined pupils with more severe and complex needs who were considered likely to require statements (HOC 1993: vol. II, p. 214).

Kent LEA, in its evidence to the House of Commons Education Committee (HOC 1993; vol. II, p. 171), did not consider statements to be an efficient way to allocate resources. The authority introduced a scheme in which six levels of support were specified. Schools were expected to complete a form for each pupil with special educational needs. Levels 1 to 3 were to be met by schools from within their allocated resources while levels 3 to 6 were to be triggers for formal assessment and possible LEA action.

Nottinghamshire LEA's scheme operated at five levels. An important distinction was made between predictable and unpredictable needs. Predictable needs were defined as the effects of general social and educational conditions. Unpredictable needs resulted from individual disabilities and learning difficulties, for example, the admission to a school of a pupil with a significant physical disability. Resources for predictable needs were allocated by an additional special education allowance to schools, using free school meals as a basis. Other indicators of predictable needs were being studied. Resources for unpredictable needs were allocated by Mainstream Support Groups in some areas and 'families' (clusters) of schools in other areas. These groups allocated support-teacher time, non-teaching assistance and development money. They made decisions on submissions from schools and information from support services (HOC 1993: vol. II, p. 121).

Although LEAs will retain a major influence on special educational arrangements, it is by no means certain that the schemes, such as those outlined, will be practicable within the new legislative framework. Until a common funding formula is introduced, LEAs will be able to influence school budgets through their LMS and LMSS procedures. But the allocation of an increasing percentage of LEA funds to schools may reduce their ability to discriminate according to schools' needs.

Themes

There are a number of management issues which arise from the new legislative framework for education. They include:

- the respective special education responsibilities of LEAs and the FAS;
- the quality of school-based information about special educational needs and provision;
- the development of LEA criteria for statutory assessment and for making statements;

- LEA responsibilities for psychological, advisory and support teaching service;
- joint working arrangements between LEAs and other agencies.

None of these themes are new but all need to be looked at in a new context. The Acts and the Code have made principles clear but given little guidance about the development of appropriate practices. While more and more is known about conditions which give rise to needs, there is a lack of an adequate database about effective forms of provision. Indeed, the parameters of provision are still uncertain.

LEA and FAS responsibilities

Although most management functions are now delegated to primary and secondary schools, it is the responsibility of LEAs and the FAS to determine school funding and to ensure that an adequate number of school places of all kinds is available. The EA 1993 gives the Secretary of State powers to make the FAS jointly responsible with an LEA or wholly responsible for providing sufficient school places. The order made may relate to primary or secondary education or both. For the Secretary of State to make an order for joint responsibility, not less than 10 per cent of pupils must be registered in grant-maintained schools. For an order making the FAS solely responsible, not less than 75 per cent of pupils must be registered in grant-maintained schools.

The Funding Agency for Schools

The FAS will become responsible for special education either when a special school achieves grant-maintained status or when the Agency sets up a new grant-maintained special school with the agreement of the LEA and Secretary of State. The FAS can, however, influence and contribute to special educational provision in a number of ways. Its policies and priorities may influence the quality of education offered to less successful and harder to teach pupils. The inadequate education of these groups often gives rise to special educational needs. In addition, there are a number of practical ways of influencing provision which include:

- the degree of specialization and selection promoted in grant-maintained schools;
- the extent to which the agency provided capital grants for access to schools;
- the size of the notional special education element in block grants to the schools it funds;
- the extent to which grant-maintained special schools are provided.

Both LEAs and the FAS may be responsible for special schools. LEAs will be responsible for LEA-maintained special schools and the FAS for grant-maintained special schools. It is assumed that, even when the FAS becomes solely responsible for primary and secondary education in an area, LEAs will continue to be responsible for LEA-maintained special schools.

The Local Education Authority

The LEA remains responsible for securing special education for children who are the subject of statements. They are expected to:

- carry out statutory assessment procedures when reasonably requested to do so by parents and schools;
- decide whether or not to make a statement of needs and provision;
- secure and pay for the provision specified in any statements made.

Each LEA will be expected to have a policy, in line with the Code, which sets out:

- the criteria to be used when deciding whether to make statutory assessments;
- the criteria to be used to decide whether to make a statement;
- the psychological and support-teaching services made available by the LEA for the purposes of assessment and for making any provision specified in statements;
- the range of provision from which parents can make a choice.

As already indicated, responsibilities for facilities and services in a range of provision for children, with and without statements, are fragmented. For example:

- advisory and support-teaching services to primary and secondary schools may be provided by an LEA or by independent contractors;
- facilities in both LEA-maintained and grant-maintained schools (special units and classes) may be authorized and financed by LEAs;
- special schools may be:
  - (a) maintained and financed by LEAs;
  - (b) grant-maintained and financed by the FAS;
  - (c) non-maintained and run by charities;
  - (d) independent and approved by the Secretary of State.

Among questions to be addressed are:

- whether competition and choice will result in an adequate range of provision;
- whether choice without planning will result in provision of quality;
- how an LEA can encourage the development and maintenance of an

adequate range of provision, and thus choice for parents, as a purchaser in a market of semi-independent providers financed from different sources.

School-based information about needs and provision

Schools will be expected to make available two kinds of information. They will be required to provide a written special education policy statement, the general form of which is prescribed in regulations, and an annual report to parents describing the implementation of the policy. Schools will also produce assessment reports and individual education plans as required by the first three stages specified in the Code of Practice. This information will be available to LEAs on request or when schools refer children for statutory assessment. Both LEA-maintained and grant-maintained schools are required to provide it. The main problem for the LEA will be the quality and reliability of the information, since policies and provision will only be evaluated by inspection every four years and annual reports will be made to parents, not the LEA. LEAs will have no basis on which to check the criteria used by individual schools to determine needs or to evaluate the provision they make.

There will apparently be no recognized qualification for SEN coordinators who may, in some schools, be senior managers without special education experience. SEN coordinators will be expected to collate information about individuals and submit reports to LEAs about children referred. Schools will be expected to have special education expertise available and staff able to prepare individual education programmes.

In practice, LEAs will have little direct evidence about a school's use of the resources available for special education. Although funding formulae include a notional percentage for special education, there is little guidance about its use. It is often difficult for staff to know what funds are available and whether an appropriate percentage is spent on special education. Recent evidence shows that many referrals for statutory assessment are triggered to obtain more resources and do not reflect the level of special educational needs within a school (Evans *et al.* 1994a).

LEA criteria for statutory assessment and statements

If the number of statements is to be kept to a minimum, it will be important to ensure that school resources are used effectively and that LEAs are kept informed about the nature and quality of the provision being made by schools. Because the information received by LEAs may vary in quality, Stages 3 and 4 in the Code provide a number of opportunities for conflicts of interest between schools and LEAs. At this stage,

LEAs have a number of options. Before making a statutory assessment, they can:

- require more information from the school;
- suggest alternative approaches to the child's difficulties based on using the school's existing resources;
- supply additional equipment to the school;
- provide support services to the school.

The Code gives general guidance, but it will be up to each LEA to develop precise criteria for initiating assessment. Easily explained procedures may help, but school and parental pressure may be important factors. Having made an assessment, the LEA must then decide whether or not to make a statement. The reasons for deciding not to make a statement will have to be very convincing if parents and schools are to be satisfied. Tribunal decisions may eventually have a significant influence on LEA practices and criteria.

In summary, LEAs will only have an indirect influence on the early detection and assessment of special educational needs and on provision for those pupils whose needs do not require a statement. They will only become directly responsible for provision after a statement is made.

Criteria for statements

The House of Commons Committee enquiry (HOC 1993) was primarily concerned with the current value of statements. The evidence received strongly supported their continued use. It was not, however, consistent about the appropriateness of statements for all kinds of needs. Most witnesses agreed that statements were appropriate for severe and complex physical and sensory disabilities and for severe learning difficulties. Parents and voluntary organizations pointed out inconsistencies in LEA practices and hoped that national criteria would be specified. Some witnesses had their doubts about the relevance of statements for pupils with emotional and behaviour difficulties. This was because procedures did not bring help quickly enough and because special education procedures became confused with exclusion procedures for disruptive pupils (HOC 1993: vol. II, p. 71).

The EA 1993 reaffirms that special education means 'educational provision which is additional to, or otherwise different from, the provision made generally for children of . . . [the child's] age in schools maintained by the local education authority or grant maintained schools in the area.' A major question remains, namely who will be in a position to know about 'the provision made generally' in an area? The Code of Practice sets out very general criteria for statements. The DFE sees the Code as providing non-binding criteria to be observed in spirit but gives little indication about how the effectiveness of proposed criteria might be monitored. There appears to be a reliance on governors of schools, parental action and infrequent inspections.

Statements and provision

The House of Commons Committee evidence (HOC 1993) indicates strong links between a statement of needs and the availability of provision. The accessibility of resources appeared to be influencing the number of referrals for statutory assessment, decisions to make a statement and the nature of the provision specified in statements. While the relationship between needs and provision is important, needs were not always being recorded in full, and in some cases, were being determined by available provision.

The Committee received little evidence that financial restraints were recognized in the field of special education and, apart from administrators, there was general support among those giving evidence for the proposition that the statement should identify all needs and that these should be met. The addendum to DES Circular 22/89 (DES 1989) recommends that all a child's needs should be recorded together with the provision to meet them. In practice, a statement may authorize:

- a placement in a special school or unit;
- special services for an individual, such as therapies and specialist teaching;
- resources to support access to the curriculum, such as non-teaching assistance or technology; and/or,
- specific educational programmes.

There seems to be a case for separating the specification of objectives from the development of individual programmes by those who are responsible for achieving the objectives. There remains uncertainty about the contractual obligations of a statement for the LEA, for the managers of schools, for providers of services and for parents. A number of questions must be answered:

- does a statement of needs imply that all needs must be met?
- would needs be more clearly specified if it was recognized that the LEA had no obligation to meet all needs at an optimum level?
- how can the obligation to meet needs and parental demands for optimum provision be reconciled with equity in provision and the efficient and cost-effective use of resources?

Psychological, advisory and support teaching services

The post-war development of special education has led to a steady increase in the employment of educational psychologists by LEAs as they assumed greater responsibilities for LEA assessment procedures. They spent a considerable proportion of their time advising and supporting teachers in primary and secondary schools and training them to meet needs. Many important initiatives in assessment and programme planning have stemmed from psychological services.

Over the same period, special education teachers were becoming more qualified and expanding their work to include advice for teachers and support for children with special educational needs in regular schools. One of the interesting outcomes of the Warnock Report and the interest in integration was the transformation of separate remedial teaching and other specialist teaching services into comprehensive support services for schools.

At the time of the House of Commons enquiry, the evidence was strongly supportive of the value of advisory and support teaching services. However, respondents could provide little data about an appropriate scale of provision or of the effectiveness of different methods of working. There was considerable concern about the effects of the proposed legislation on the ability of LEAs to continue to make comprehensive services available. As a result, some changes were made in the 1993 Education Bill to make provision for psychological and education welfare services, a mandatory exception from delegation under LMS. However, the effect of the EA 1993 has been to fragment responsibilities which overlap at Stage 3 of the Code's assessment procedures.

Primary and secondary schools are expected to select and to specify the services they propose to employ to support work with the children for which they are responsible. These can be purchased in the market or supplied by LEAs under contract to do so. Purchasing support services is a very different financial burden for large and small schools. The ability to afford proper levels of support will depend on a number of factors including the school's catchment area, budget, and level of staff expertise. Further comment on financing services appears in Chapter 8.

The future development of psychological and support-teaching services in the new financial and legislative framework is uncertain. Little has been said about the nature and extent of services which may be necessary. No steps have been taken to ensure the quality standards of independent commercial providers of services.

Inter-agency collaboration

The EA 1993 makes some attempt to encourage inter-agency cooperation. It states that:

> When it appears to a local authority that any District Health Authority or local authority could, by taking specific action, help

in the exercise of their functions under this part of the Act they may request the help of the authority specifying the action in question. An authority whose help is requested shall comply unless:

- other authorities consider the help requested not necessary for the functions exercised by the LEA;
- the Health Authority, having regard to resources, considers the request unreasonable;
- the local authority consider the request is incompatible with their own duties and obligations (DFE 1993, Section 166).

It is easy to see that many reasons can be found for non-compliance with LEA requests and that inter-agency cooperation will remain difficult and limited. At the local authority level, education and social services departments have many overlapping interests particularly in provision for children under five, children with special needs in primary, secondary and special schools, and in the period of transition from school to adult life.

Social services responsibilities are set out in the Children Act 1989 (DoH 1989), which requires them to register and meet special needs. They are also required by the Disabled Persons Act 1986 (DHSS 1986) to make post-school provision. A lack of clarity in definitions makes for uncertainty, and limited resources make inter-agency cooperation hard to implement.

Some difficulties which arise are concerned with the specification and implementation of the non-educational provision specified in statements. Others arise because of shared responsibilities for meeting children's needs which are on the borderline between agency responsibilities. Because definitions of disability in health and social security legislation are not compatible with the EA 1993 definitions, agencies are not responsible for the same populations. It is relatively easy for other agencies to say that a child who is the subject of a statement does not fall within the groups of children to whose needs they are required to make a contribution.

A more significant point is the general lay assumption that special education includes a variety of therapies provided by health services. Different agency responsibilities are recognized in the Code, but the persistence of a medical model encourages the belief that therapies are an integral part of provision. Those concerned with disability are familiar with these issues as they occur from birth to senescence and have not been solved in any phase of life.

Borderline problems are also concerned with how an agency defines its clients and activities. Children in the care of local authorities often have educational difficulties but agreement between education and social service departments about which children should be the subject of statements is not always easy. The same is true of behaviour problems and how to deal with them. For example, are the distinctions between behaviour difficulties and delinquency clear, and how should LEAs and social services work together to solve them?

There are other central inter-agency issues. Each authority will have its own policies and priorities. Health services may be more concerned with adult than children's services. Planning and budget cycles may be different, making it difficult to finance provision jointly. Staff may be unfamiliar with the procedures and requirements of other agencies.

Policy development and coordination

The government expects local agencies to demonstrate coordinated policy development, but each central department appears to go its own way and there are few effective measures to ensure cooperation. The Minister for the Disabled has information about the activities of departments, but no powers to see that there is a coherent approach to disability. Even within departments, such as the DFE, special education can be an afterthought as the ERA 1988 demonstrated.

The new framework for special education is in place, but the contributions of other departments to its implementation are assumed rather than specified. There are guidelines for effective inter-agency work at local authority level, but, unless senior officers in education, health and social services take coordination seriously, junior staff will not have the time or the resources to enable them to work together.

Local government

The current review of local government may result in a few more small unitary authorities, but, in many instances, a two-tier arrangement will continue. The effects of the review have been to create some uncertainty and to inhibit the implementation of legislation. The provision of a reasonable range of choice for parents in a region will not be easy unless authorities coordinate their policies and work closely with the FAS. There appears to be a need for some form of regional or sub-regional committee to look at gaps and overlaps in facilities and services.

Conclusion

It is hard to avoid the conclusion that a policy designed to enhance parental choice and the independence of individual schools has made it more difficult to ensure that there is an adequate range of special educational facilities and support services.

7 Post-16 Further and Continuing Education

Until the end of the 1980s, schools and further education colleges were part of a common education system administered by local education authorities. The FHEA 1992 created a post-16 market in which relatively independent schools and colleges are expected to compete for students. Although working within nationally determined curriculum and qualification frameworks, they are responsible for their own management. The competing providers of post-16 education and vocational training include:

- sixth forms in secondary schools financed by either the LEA or FAS;
- sixth form, tertiary and further education colleges primarily financed by the Further Education Funding Council (FEFC);
- training organizations financed by local Training and Enterprise Councils (TECs).

Secondary schools continue to offer traditional GCSEs and 'A' levels but they can now offer courses leading to vocational qualifications. Colleges also offer both academic and vocational courses. Training and Enterprise Councils finance vocational preparation and training courses run by colleges and other training organizations. Post-16 financing is increasingly dependent on student numbers and the outcomes of their studies. The FHEA 1992 separates vocational and non-vocational post-school education. LEAs continue to be responsible for adult education which may be provided by Adult Education Institutes or by colleges.

One of the requirements of the legislation is that the FEFC should ensure that further education is available to all and that vocational proficiency is improved. It is specifically charged to see that facilities and services are provided for students with disabilities and learning difficulties. The development of a coherent policy to meet the needs of children, young people and adults with such disabilities and difficulties, from the early years to adulthood, involves post-16 provision of all kinds. This chapter looks briefly at the history of such arrangements and the opportunities offered to such students in the new post-16 market.

The background

Although some voluntary organizations made post-school arrangements for young people with disabilities and learning difficulties, relatively little provision was made in maintained colleges of further education before the Warnock Report. That Report made post-16 provision one of its three priority areas and stimulated considerable development in the maintained sector. A Bureau for Handicapped Students, now Skill, was set up, and many colleges developed provision. Arrangements were given further impetus in London by an ILEA policy designed to improve what was locally known as Level 2 provision (ILEA 1985). Subsequent work by the Further Education Unit (FEU 1989a, 1989b) stimulated a number of important curriculum initiatives.

Provision at the time took one of three forms:

- arrangements to support individuals taking regular college courses;
- bridging courses to enable students to follow regular college courses;
- discrete special courses for groups of students with particular disabilities.

During the 1970s and 1980s, special schools also paid more attention to post-16 needs. A number of post-16 units were set up in maintained special schools. Voluntary organizations also developed further education units in non-maintained special schools in addition to specialist post-16 colleges. It is important to note that LEAs did not set up separate maintained further education provision for young people with special educational needs. It slowly became recognized as a responsibility of further education colleges.

By the time that the FHEA 1992 was passed, most colleges were making some provision for students with disabilities and learning difficulties. There was also a developing network of lecturers with knowledge and experience of work with these students and an increasing amount of appropriate curriculum material.

The new framework

The government's aims for further education embodied in the White Paper *Education and Training for the 21st Century* (DES 1991) and in the subsequent FHEA 1992 were to:

- increase participation;
- improve standards;
- prepare young people and adults for an effective working life.

These priorities are now being implemented. The FHEA 1992 makes a distinction between vocational and non-vocational education, categorizing adult education as non-vocational. A number of definitions are set out in Schedule 2 of the Act. Vocational provision includes:

- vocational qualification courses approved by the Secretary of State;
- general certificate of education and advanced general certificates;
- courses approved by the Secretary of State which prepare for entry to higher education;
- courses in basic literacy;
- courses to teach the basic principles of mathematics;
- courses to teach independent living and communication skills to persons having learning difficulties which prepare them for other courses falling within the schedule.

The FHEA 1992 was the first to establish provision for students with disabilities and learning difficulties as an integral part of further education. The final item on the schedule is of particular importance to such students. However, the separation of further and adult or continuing education is thought by many to limit opportunities for students with complex and profound learning difficulties. Competition for students and outcome-related funding (in other words, payment by results) are unlikely to be particularly helpful to them.

Adult and continuing education

Although this chapter is primarily concerned with further education, it is important to recognize the past contribution of adult and continuing education and its potential to contribute to the personal development and education of many young people and adults with a wide variety of special needs. Prior to recent legislation, adult and continuing education made a considerable impact through literacy and numeracy programmes and other ways of improving access to further education. A period in a non-vocational adult education class often re-established confidence and learning habits so that the individual could enter vocational education.

Adult education provided in hospitals and training centres also made significant provision for adults with severe disabilities. Preparation for more independent living in the community and preparation for possible employment, were and are valuable elements in adult education programmes. This aspect of adult education has not received the recognition it deserves.

This DFE approach to non-vocational education may limit opportunities for the development of social and life skills. It may encourage premature judgements about future employment of those with severe disabilities and limit the opportunities open to them. It is unfortunate that the vocational/non-vocational divide, discussed later, seems to envisage adult education as self-financing leisure learning for those who can afford it.

The nature of further education

Unlike schools, colleges do not have an overall curriculum framework within which to deliver their wide range of courses and, until relatively recently, they had few direct curriculum responsibilities. Colleges were expected to deliver a range of courses to achieve national qualifications for which the syllabuses, examinations and standards were determined by professional and examining bodies. They were primarily concerned with curriculum delivery (McGinty and Fish 1993). Their main concern was the vocational preparation of young people in the 16–19 age range. Students were selected for admission and emphasis was placed on levels of work. The higher the level of work and qualification, the higher the salary scale of the staff concerned. More recently, the age range of students has extended and now reflects the age distribution of the population as a whole. College programmes and their delivery have become much more sensitive to the different backgrounds and needs of students from sixteen to sixty plus. Greater attention is now paid to curriculum development and delivery.

Colleges are providing courses financed by the FEFC, Training and Enterprise Councils (TECs), employers and other bodies, which expect to influence programme development and delivery. At the same time, a national system of vocational qualifications is being introduced. Expectations for colleges are set out in a framework for inspection produced by the FEFC. A number of positive features which inspectors might hope to see in a good college are outlined. Under the heading of 'Responsiveness and range of provision' are:

- awareness of national policies and targets;
- effective liaison with employers, schools, parents, the community and other FE and HE institutions;

- a range of programmes which meet the needs of potential clients;
- access to and participation in further education for under-represented groups.

Under the heading of 'teaching and the promotion of learning', staff should:

- challenge and extend students' skill, knowledge and understanding;
- encourage their personal development;
- take account of the different abilities of students on a programme;
- set learning in a context of what has gone before;
- choose a variety of teaching and learning approaches.

Generously interpreted, these guidelines facilitate the inclusion of students with disabilities and learning difficulties in the college programme.

Vocational and non-vocational education

The FHEA 1992 was preoccupied with improving national vocational proficiency. Broadly speaking, anything which enhances employability is vocational further education. Anything related to personal leisure and recreation is non-vocational adult education. This distinction is proving disadvantageous to the education and training of students with disabilities. One result is to characterize what is described as personal and social education as non-vocational. Yet for many, including those with disabilities and learning difficulties, effective personal and social education enhances employment prospects. There are as many jobs lost for lack of personal skills as for lack of vocational ones.

Students with disabilities and learning difficulties

Educational objectives for colleges should encompass provision for a wide range of students, including those with disabilities and learning difficulties. Young people with special educational needs leave school between the ages of 16 and 19. The development of post-16 units in schools means individuals may come to college with very different levels of social and educational proficiency. Most students with severe and complex needs will have been the subject of statements. However, it is important for colleges to recognize that a number of young people acquire disabilities later in life through trauma and accidents.

A further education contribution to the individual should be set in a context of what has gone before and what will come afterwards. This context is concerned with the final years in school, transition planning, interagency cooperation and post-college arrangements (McGinty and Fish 1992).

Assessment of needs

The Code of Practice identifies a number of assessments during adolescence. Apart from educational assessments, parallel assessments are required by the Chronic Sick and Disabled Persons Act 1970 (DHSS 1970), the Disabled Persons Act 1986 (DHSS 1986), the Children Act 1989 (DoH 1989) and the NHS and Community Care Act 1990 (DoH 1990). Arrangements should be made to enable these assessments to draw from and contribute to the review process required by the Code. There are two educational assessments to consider: assessment leading to a personal transition plan, as set out in the Code and assessment on entry to college to identify learning and support needs in that context.

The Code states that the LEA is responsible for the 14+ review of statements and must ensure that other providers, such as social services, are aware of the review. 'The first annual review after a young person's 14th birthday and any subsequent reviews until the child leaves school, should include a transition plan which will draw together information . . . in order to plan coherently for the young person's transition to adult life' (p. 117).

The Code goes on to outline the nature of the transition programme and the people who should be involved in its development. It recognizes that further education should be an element in most programmes. The outcome of assessment will depend on a combination of parent and student choice with professional recommendations. Choice may also be influenced by colleges anxious to maintain or increase student numbers. Schools, in particular special schools, may wish to retain individuals as long as possible. They may minimize the value of moving to the more adult college atmosphere. Parents may be influenced by the need to protect their children and choose small separate specialist provision rather than colleges.

Having decided to apply to a college, potential students will face further assessment either by colleges or agents authorized by them. Such assessments will be concerned with whether the college has appropriate programmes and the learner and learning support arrangements necessary for the student. The transition period is a difficult one for individuals and their families. The Code initiative is positive, but unless the other agencies support a single transition plan, provision may be piecemeal and ineffective. If there are no clear LEA policies, if professionals are not well informed about transition and if resources are limited, inadequate programmes may be a result.

Transition from school

During the 1980s, considerable international attention was devoted to the transition of young people with disabilities and learning difficulties from school, through further education and vocational preparation, to an adult working life. The Centre for Educational Research and Innovation (CERI) of the Organization for Economic Cooperation and Development (OECD) undertook a major study. A number of reports were published on the nature of transition and successful means of effecting it (OECD/CERI 1986, 1988, 1991, 1994). The work stressed the importance of continuity in programmes from school, through post-school provision and preparation for employment to entry to work and independent living. Other themes were the need for information and guidance, inter-agency cooperation and the management of individual transition.

Transition programmes for young people, including those who are disabled whatever the nature and degree of their disabilities, should work towards the same objectives. There is a need for broadly agreed objectives to be accepted by all agencies, professionals, young people and their parents. Any modification of these objectives should take place only after young people have had education, training and work experience. Opportunities for further education and training should not be restricted by premature judgements about future employment.

The Further Education Unit (FEU 1989c) carried out a programme of research in association with OECD. It identified the need to work with parents and professionals to establish adult status, emphasized the contribution of technology and stressed the importance of supported employment. In the UK context, the contribution of further education colleges was seen as crucial to transition both in terms of developing adult skills and preparing for employment. A number of developments have made it more difficult to develop and support individual transition plans:

- the separation of responsibilities for schools from those for colleges;
- delegated management to schools and colleges;
- the creation of a post-16 market;
- end-product-related funding.

Inter-agency cooperation

Inter-agency cooperation is essential if effective transition plans are to be put into effect. At national level, government departments develop policies in relative isolation one from another. There is little evidence of awareness of the effects of one department's policy on another, for example, the relationship of LEA statements to Children Act registers of special needs and eligibility criteria for disability benefits and allowances. There is a need to coordinate contributions to meeting individual and family needs. There also needs to be a recognition that transition is a shared responsibility for education, health, employment, social services, housing and other departments. Consistent and compatible terminology and criteria for disability are necessary as are clear guidelines which set out priorities, define responsibilities and nominate the service expected to coordinate the implementation of transition arrangements. At the local authority level, each sector is often ignorant about the policies and priorities of other sectors. More attention needs to be given to joint consultation and planning.

The college contribution

Much needs to be done by local authority agencies, potential students and their families to arrange entry to an appropriate college and to ensure adequate financial support, particularly for students with significant care needs being educated away from home. Students and their families are faced with a choice between provision in specialist colleges, which cater for students with disabilities, and local colleges of further education. There is a small group of about 120 colleges, which set out to provide specialist courses for students with marked disabilities and learning difficulties. Around 30 of them are members of a National Association. At their best, they integrate a further education programme with an independent living programme within a 24-hour curriculum. Although having specialist strengths, these colleges can become isolated. An increasing number are now forging links with local colleges to overcome this problem and to extend the range of opportunities they can offer.

College programmes now have to include arrangements to support learning and other provision for students with disabilities and learning difficulties. Experience suggests that the educational needs of these students are best met within an inclusive college-wide framework, which takes into account a range of special needs. Colleges need to develop support for learning to encourage a wider range of students to profit from further education (FEU 1992). *Support for learning* has two main components – learner support and learning support: (i) *learner support* is concerned with guidance, counselling and the provision of facilities and services, such as personal care arrangements which enable a student to follow a programme of study; (ii) *learning support* is concerned with the tutorial and other help individuals may need, including the development of basic skills, to facilitate their learning.

Appropriate support for learning enables students with special needs to have greater access to colleges. In addition, learner and learning support provision tends to take three main forms:

- support for individual students on regular courses;
- modules to prepare students for college courses;
- separate courses for particular disabilities and needs.

At the time of writing a Committee, under the chairmanship of Professor Tomlinson, set up by the FEFC was looking at the further education provision of students with disabilities and/or learning difficulties. It is considering a number of aspects of provision including the assessment of student needs, the support they require and curriculum development. The Committee is expected to report in 1995.

Post-school issues

The importance of continuity in provision and of collaboration between agencies during transition has already been emphasized. By introducing a national curriculum for schools and a national system of vocational qualifications, the new framework has brought some coherence to what is being delivered. But the creation of national standards can also unwittingly increase the handicaps faced by some students with disabilities. The post-16 market also creates problems because there are no incentives to take students who are harder to teach, who cost more, and who may take longer to achieve recognized qualifications. The emphasis on end-product financing also reduces attention to the quality of further education and to the 'value-added' element.

Problems which face potential students with special needs include:

- whether to stay on in school;
- how to ensure appropriate post-school supporting arrangements;
- whether to choose a specialist or regular college;
- how to finance further education.

Staying on until 18+, often in a relatively small special school, has some advantages. Provision specified in statements can be assured. There are no increased costs to families and the early stages of transition can be handled in collaboration with the local authority department. There are, however, disadvantages. The pace of work and the demands of schools may not be good preparation for further education. Adequate planning for the next phase may not take place. Above all, the young person may not be educated in an environment which encourages increased maturity and a more adult approach to learning.

Entry to further education will be facilitated by the proposals in the

Code of Practice for assessment and inter-agency planning. But the transition assessment made will need to be supplemented by a specific assessment of the support required by the individual in a particular college. The choice of college, college admission procedures and preparation for entry are all hurdles to be overcome. Although much will depend on college policies, active and informed support by LEAs and social services will often be crucial.

Further education and training has to be set within a programme which enables the individual to prepare for life in his or her community which is as independent and self-supporting as possible. The choice between specialist and other colleges is not easy. Specialist colleges can provide multi-professional programmes. Because many are residential, they can provide a 24-hour curriculum in which independent living and vocational preparation are integrated. On the other hand, unless they are in touch with the students' homes, it may be more difficult to integrate them back into their local communities. Unless specialist colleges are in close contact with other colleges, their programmes may not always reflect current further education standards.

The question of financial support for post-school education is a difficult one. The student with help often has to put together a package consisting of disability allowances, social service support for living and educational support for learning. What may seem administratively tidy presents a student with an endless series of forms to be filled in and a reluctance in some cases to make a contribution.

The strong vocational emphasis on college provision also makes it more difficult to gain access and financial support for students with severe and profound disabilities and learning difficulties. There is a tendency to make judgements about possible outcomes and employability without giving the individual a trial. There is also a lack of recognition that social and life skills are essential to employability and a reluctance to finance programmes because they do not appear vocational. Finally, the separation of further education from adult education has made a lifelong educational support programme for individuals with disabilities much harder to implement.

Current issues

As with other provision, further education is currently at the mercy of a government short-term, cost-cutting policy. Responsibilities for the future development of further education are uncertain. The Further Education Staff College (FESC) and the Further Education Unit (FEU) are being merged under the aegis of the FEFC. Both have made a contribution to the field with the FEU playing a significant part in the development of curricula and provision for students with disabilities and learning difficulties. It is hard to see where disinterested comment and advice about further education and special provision will come from in the future.

If the transition requirements of the Code are implemented, further education will become part of an integrated programme for the individual to which different agencies contribute. But individuals will need advice and guidance. The contribution that the new careers service will be able to make is not yet clear. It will be important that those responsible for assessment and advice at this point in an individual's life, do not make premature judgements about outcomes. Judgements about adult lifelong possibilities must be delayed until a reasonable transition programme has been completed.

There are a number of issues facing practitioners who are working with the students concerned. These include:

- a lack of senior management knowledge and interest in students with disabilities and learning difficulties;
- the incompatibility of FEFC aspirations with many college practices;
- the balance of integrated and separate provision;
- curriculum development for those with severe learning difficulties which meet their needs and comply with vocational objectives;
- the development of accredited modules or courses which facilitate access to the first levels of national qualifications.

It would be useful if an accurate audit of student needs was carried out in colleges. As in the case of schools, it would be helpful if provision for students with common learning support needs were distinguished from provision for students whose disabilities are assessed to require individual programmes for learner and learning support. Meeting most learning support needs should be an integral part of college provision for all students. The number of students who would require individual education and care packages could then be kept to a minimum.

Conclusion

The provision of further education for students with disabilities and learning difficulties is important for the economy. It will enable some of them to enter employment and to contribute through taxation. But it is equally important to recognize that effective further education can reduce long-term costs by increasing autonomy and promoting independent living. If these young people are to be accepted as adults, the same quality standards applied throughout colleges should be applied rigorously to this area of work. They are devalued by being patronized and their future is blighted by low-standard provision. There are a number of key questions to be answered about meeting their needs in further education. It is important to know how far improvements in accessibility and inclusiveness in regular colleges will meet the needs of students with disabilities and learning difficulties and how far separate provision will be necessary.

The relationship between inclusive provision within colleges and separate provision for these students elsewhere needs to be clarified and the best qualities of effective, discrete provision disseminated in colleges. Funding mechanisms which ensure that further education provision is accessible and inclusive are required. Colleges should also encourage and support the development of personal, social and life skills. But the most significant issue is how to implement effective transition plans, which include appropriate further education, in a post-16 market and how to coordinate contributions to plans from all the different agencies involved.

8 / Funding Special Education

The recent changes in the funding of primary, secondary and special schools have brought into clearer focus a number of issues which were always inherent in resourcing special educational needs. These are:

1 Are needs best resourced *individually* (through statements), or *collectively* (through a general allocation to schools to allow them to meet the needs of all the pupils in their area)?
2 How are the needs to be identified and how are decisions to be taken about the amount of resources needed to support them?
3 What is the most effective mechanism for allocating resources to schools or pupils?
4 How can accountability for the use of resources be ensured?
5 How can an evaluation of the cost-effectiveness of various forms of provision be undertaken?

This chapter will discuss these questions from within the current framework of LMS, LMSS and GMS and suggest a possible framework for the future.

The impact of LMS, LMSS and GMS on funding special educational provision

Local management of schools (LMS) consists of a 'package of measures' (Thomas 1990) which includes the following elements: formula-funding, open enrolment and site-based management. The driving force behind LMS is the desire of the government to open up the public sector to 'market forces', and within the education service (as well as other services such as health and housing) to produce an 'internal market' to stimulate efficiency and effectiveness. Commentators (Lee 1992; Evans and Lunt 1994; Lunt and Evans 1994) have suggested that pupils with special educational needs will be vulnerable within the educational market-place.

Formula funding of schools was phased in over four years between 1990 and 1994. The formula by which schools are funded has to be 'simple, clear and predictable in its impact' (DES 1988a). It has to be based primarily on pupil numbers weighted by age. There is scope, also, to include some weightings for special educational needs, and these have been used to a greater or lesser extent by LEAs in devising their formulae. Circular 7/88 (DES 1988a) also defined *mandatory* and *discretionary* exceptions to delegation, which consisted of services which LEAs were permitted to fund centrally. Such exceptions included many of the services which support pupils with special educational needs, for example, the psychology service, support-teaching teams, and funding for pupils with statements.

LMS and formula-funding have undergone several revisions since 1988, and are currently governed by Circular 2/94 (DFE 1994h). This Circular also covers the Local Management of Special Schools (LMSS), introduced in April 1994. Currently, a minimum of 75 per cent of the funding of primary and secondary schools must be allocated on the basis of age-weighted pupil numbers. The remainder can be allocated on the basis of 'other factors' which include: small school curriculum protection; small school salary protection; premises costs; and, 'additional educational needs'. This latter term appears to cover those whom we have termed 'the harder to teach' – pupils whose special educational needs are not considered to require a statement – and other additional educational needs, such as 'social deprivation'. It may also cover the costs of pupils who are the subject of statements if LEAs decide to delegate these to schools. The Circular calls for 'criteria' for the identification of pupils without statements and those with additional educational needs and specification of the basis upon which resources will be allocated. The Circular states that:

> The purpose of formula funding is to bring about an equitable allocation of resources as between schools, based on objectively measured

> needs rather than historical spending patterns. Within each LEA, schools with the same characteristics and the same number of pupils should receive the same level of resources under the formula.
> (p. 7, para. 7)

However, the search for 'objective' criteria for the allocation of resources has shown them to be rather elusive (Lee 1992). LEAs are using a wide range of methods of resource allocation, both for age-weightings (Thomas and Bullock 1994) and for SEN weightings (HOC 1993; Lunt and Evans 1994). These will be discussed in more detail below.

Circular 2/94 (DFE 1994h), dealing with LMSS, sets out the way in which the formula for special schools and units is to be constructed. It differs significantly from the LMS formula for primary and secondary schools in that it is based on a *place element* rather than on age-weighted pupil numbers. That is, special schools are funded on the basis of the number of places they offer for particular types of need, whether or not those places are filled. This is to enable a 'stable resource base to be maintained, whilst still allowing for the admission of pupils whose needs are identified during the year' (para. 114). LMSS schemes can also contain an element of funding for 'outreach' work to enable special schools to work with primary and secondary schools to support their special educational provision and to enhance opportunities for integration.

LEAs have differed in their approaches to the challenge of producing LMSS schemes. Some have attempted to integrate their schemes for LMS and LMSS to produce a range of levels of resourcing for pupils with SEN in mainstream and special school setting. Northamptonshire LEA, for example, has a scheme which provides a continuum ranging from support within the mainstream classroom to full-time placement in a special school or unit. Kent LEA is developing a method of auditing special needs, which allocates resources to pupils with and without statements on the basis of cost of their placement in primary and secondary schools. Some other LEAs have made no attempt to link the funding of mainstream and special schools, nor to create some kind of continuum. These LEAs appear to see the resourcing of special education as a separate endeavour from that of resourcing primary and secondary schools.

LEAs also differ in their approaches to funding special educational provision in GM schools. Provision for pupils with statements in those schools is to be funded by the LEA. However, problems may arise when a statutory assessment indicates that a child in a GM school should be jointly funded by the school and the LEA. Pupils whose special educational needs are not the subject of statements may not be entitled to support from LEA services if the money for these has already been notionally delegated to the GM school as part of its share of centrally held funds. Some LEAs are very hardline on this issue and will not offer any support to GM schools. Others are more pragmatic, and will offer support on the basis that (a) if they do not, pupils will suffer and (b) preventative support at an early stage may obviate the need for a statement (which the LEA would have to fund).

It is likely, when the FAS begins to take on some funding responsibilities through the Common Funding Formula (CFF), that the situation will become even more complex. The CFF funding allocations in an area may not bear any relation to the LEA funding arrangements for SEN. LEAs will therefore be obliged to provide different levels of service to LEA and GM schools. It remains to be seen whether the number of statements in GM schools will increase once the CFF starts to operate. There is still a great deal of confusion about the respective responsibilities of LEAs and the governors of GM and LEA schools for funding and making provision for special educational needs. These responsibilities may have to be further tested in the courts in order to get some clarification.

The impact of LMS on centrally funded support services

LEAs have adopted a number of approaches to the provision of support services for SEN. Some LEAs have managed to maintain a full range of support services which schools can access on the basis of some form of referral procedure. Others have cut considerably the range of services they are offering in order to stay within the government-imposed limits for centrally retained funds. Most vulnerable to these cuts have been teams of advisory teachers for the less severe needs, such as reading support and behaviour support. Many of these teams have been disbanded and the teachers redeployed back into schools. The long-term effect of this may be an increase in the numbers of children given statements, and thus individually resourced at a greater cost (Lunt and Evans 1994). Evidence to the Select Committee suggested that teams to provide for the less common problems of sensory and physical impairment would not be disbanded, as their expertise could not be recreated in schools. It would not be cost-effective to provide such support services on anything less than an LEA-wide basis, given the incidence of such problems within the school population.

LEAs have a number of options open to them for funding support services:

1 To fund them fully from the centre and allow schools access free of charge. This would involve some kind of referral process, or gatekeeping activity. LEAs would also have to decide *which* services they want to offer.
2 To delegate funding for part or all of some services and leave schools

to buy back those which they want to make use of. The problem with this option is that if schools did not use the services then they would disappear, with consequent problems for the support of some pupils. Once again, this might lead to a rise in demand for statements.

3 To create 'agencies' to provide support services and for those agencies to market themselves to schools. These agencies would be free-standing units within the LEA structure, and would therefore be vulnerable to the decisions of schools about whether or not they wished to purchase their services.
4 To set up 'purchaser/provider' agreements between LEAs and schools where LEAs would agree to buy places on behalf of pupils with learning difficulties. This system would depend upon schools being able to provide the necessary support, which, in its turn would depend on the level of resources within the school which are partly a function of LEA funding policies. It would also depend upon the expertise and attitudes to SEN within the school, as some schools might have adequate funding, but would not make SEN provision a priority.

Each of the alternatives described above has been used by some LEAs as part of their attempts to preserve support for pupils with SEN and at the same time meet the government's requirements for delegation of funding and responsibility to schools. Some support services have disappeared under 'buy back' and 'agency' schemes, which may indicate that they were not found to be very effective by schools. Or it might indicate that schools are operating on short time-scales and have solved temporary funding problems by cutting back on special needs support without realizing that the consequences would be the disappearance of services. Psychology and Education Welfare services are now mandatory exceptions, and their funding cannot be delegated. It may be that the activities of these two services will expand to take the place of other services which have been cut back or have disappeared altogether.

Whatever arrangements for maintaining support services LEAs adopt, they need to be carefully planned and monitored to ensure that pupils still have access to the services they need.

Individual versus collective resourcing of special educational needs

At present there are several methods of resourcing special educational needs (SEN) under LMS:

1 SEN can be resourced as part of the basic Age Weighted Pupil Unit (AWPU). That is, LEAs can make it clear that the basic AWPU

contains a notional sum for 'predictable' special educational needs – those which are likely to occur in every classroom (the needs of the '18 per cent'). This method has caused problems because as the SEN element is not separately identified, some schools have tended to assume that they have not been given money for SEN, and have then attempted to gain extra funding for pupils with mild forms of learning difficulty through support services or statements.

2 On top of the basic AWPU, the LEA can allocate money on the basis of 'additional educational needs' and 'special educational needs'. These two elements can be used separately or in combination. The problem lies in deciding on criteria for identifying the extent of SEN or social needs within a school and the monetary value which should be attached to these elements. This will be discussed in more detail below, but at this point, it is important to note that the criteria for the allocation of funds can either be at a general level, using some general measure of needs such as entitlement to free school meals, or it can be at an individual level based on some individualized measure of need, such as an audit.

3 Some LEAs have allocated a sum of money for special educational needs to a cluster of schools. The rationale behind this form of allocation is that the schools in the locality would be in the best position to make use of those funds to meet exceptional special needs within their cluster group. Nottinghamshire and Wiltshire LEAs, among others, have adopted this method, and have allocated funds to groups of schools to support pupils with moderate learning difficulties, who otherwise might be the subject of a statement. This is part of an attempt to reduce, or at least contain the demand for statements, which most LEAs are finding is rising under the new funding arrangements (Lunt and Evans 1994).

4 The most individualized form of special needs resourcing is through a statement. When the 1981 Act was first implemented, it was envisaged that the statement rate would be around 1.8 per cent, the proportion of pupils then in special schools. The rate has risen inexorably over the past 10 years, and particularly in the years following the setting up of LMS. Currently the national average is around 2.4 per cent, but some LEAs are giving statements to 4 per cent of their school population. Some statement provision is very cheap; one LEA is giving schools less than £400 per annum to provide extra support for children in mainstream. Other provision, for example in highly specialized residential settings, is very expensive – £25,000 per annum or more. The question must be raised whether it is cost effective to go through the process of a statutory assessment in order to deal with relatively mild and common forms of learning difficulties which will result in small amounts of extra support in mainstream.

The point is whether schools and teachers can be expected to supply levels of expertise and resources which will enable them to provide effectively for a range of learning and behaviour difficulties which are currently, in many LEAs, supported by funding individual pupils through statements. If all schools were able to offer such expertise and were adequately resourced, then the individual identification of, and provision of a statement for large numbers of pupils might not be necessary.

How are needs to be identified and decisions taken about levels of resourcing?

The Code of Practice has laid down procedures which schools must use to identify needs in order to make provision for them. However, this begs the question of *how* and *how much* provision should be made. The Code clearly indicates that schools are expected to make provision at Stages 1–3, although they may involve external services at Stage 3. The LEA is only directly involved in provision at Stages 4 and 5. However, LEAs' decisions about how to allocate funding to schools to enable them to make provision and how much to allocate for the different levels of need are crucial to schools' abilities to meet needs. For example, should LEAs focus their attention on early intervention, and provide early years education for all 3- and 4-year-olds? Should they put massive resources into Reading Recovery programmes for 6-year-olds? Should the balance between funding for primary and secondary schools be changed, so that more resources can be concentrated at the primary level?

There is obviously a need for effective methods of identification and early intervention for pupils with learning difficulties, but this will rely on more than an elaborate set of procedures, such as those laid down in the Code. It will involve a complex series of decisions about values and priorities at the school and the LEA level: decisions about the point at which concerns about a child are translated into interventions; decisions about what type of intervention is most appropriate; decisions about the point at which a child moves from one stage to the next, and at what point the LEA might become involved.

As an example, one might take the case of a child with specific learning difficulties with reading and writing (dyslexia). Some children with this problem are provided for at minimal cost within classrooms, sometimes with the support of specially qualified teachers from an LEA team. Other children, whose parents have pursued their child's interests with the LEA, have been given access to highly specialized and highly expensive resources in segregated settings, at the LEA's expense. The Audit Commission has highlighted significant differences in levels of provision across the country and called for nationally agreed criteria. The DFE is attempting to devise a common funding formula for GM schools. However, it seems unlikely, given the range of policies and funding priorities currently in operation, that the use of *national* rather than *local* criteria will be possible.

In the last resort then, decisions about levels of resourcing are taken at the local level, by LEAs, the FAS and schools. Schools have to produce policies for parents and governors to explain their provision for SEN. LEAs are accountable to the local electorate and to the parents and governors for their policies. Nevertheless, decisions about resource allocation are influenced by a wide range of considerations other than the needs of pupils with SEN.

What is the most effective mechanism for allocating resources?

Whether it is the additional educational needs of schools, clusters or individuals which are resourced, it is still necessary to have some mechanism that will identify the level of needs and allocate resources. Currently there is a debate about whether proxy measures of special educational needs, such as free school meals, are an effective way of doing this. This goes to the heart of the debate described earlier, about the relationship between additional needs and special educational needs, and whether it is useful to distinguish between the two. Leeds LEA currently funds both special educational needs and social needs through two separate formulae, both based on free school meals. In addition, they fund a significant number of statements for pupils in mainstream schools. So they are using free school meals as a proxy measure of both special educational needs and social deprivation, as well as using some individualized assessment of SEN for some pupils.

Nottinghamshire LEA is also targeting resources for special educational needs support by using free school meals. The rationale they use to support this is that the data on free school meals are easily obtainable (although there are some queries about whether *entitlement* or *take-up* is the better indicator) and that at a school level, it is a good indicator of the general level of special educational needs within a school. However, the use of free school meals does nothing to dispel the confusion about whether the resources are to be used for pupils experiencing social deprivation (which may be most pupils in a school, depending on the catchment area) or for pupils with special educational needs, whether or not these are due to the effects of social deprivation.

Another problem with the use of free school meals (or other similar indicators, such as take up of clothing grant, or data from census returns) is that schools in relatively affluent areas receive very little support from this type of allocation, although they may have a considerable number of pupils with special educational needs. This is particularly true of schemes where there is a *threshold* below which no extra funding is given. An example would be a school which has a large proportion of children with parents in the armed services. Such children often have significant learning support needs, but would not be entitled to free school meals.

Having raised these problems, it is important to note that there are cogent arguments for the use of a proxy indicator, such as free school meals. It resources *schools* rather than individual pupils. This gives schools the freedom to use the resources as they see best to meet the needs of all their pupils. If the level of expertise and commitment in a school is sufficient, staff will have the opportunity to provide some creative solutions to children's learning problems.

A method of identifying needs and allocating resources which is becoming more common is that of an *audit* of schools. The DFE was originally opposed to this method as it relied on teachers' judgements and was therefore not seen as sufficiently 'objective'. The Special Needs Audit was pioneered by Kent LEA, although currently there are a number of LEAs using similar approaches. It involves the individual identification of children within a school who need varying levels of support or intervention because of their special educational needs. The Kent scheme originally had three levels: support from the class teacher, support from an SEN teacher and support from an external source. These are similar to levels 1–3 within the Code of Practice. Kent has now extended its scheme to six levels, to include pupils with statements. In order to overcome the problems of 'objectivity' the audit returns are moderated by a team of headteachers from within the area of the schools concerned, along with an advisory teacher. Resource allocations are then made on the basis of the numbers of pupils in a school with different levels of need.

A major advantage of this approach is that it appears to raise the levels of awareness in schools about pupils with SEN, and it focuses teachers' minds on exactly what are an individual child's needs and what level of support is required. There could be a problem with 'over-identification' because of the needs of schools to maximize their income. However, this should be balanced by the moderation procedures and also by the knowledge that schools' Standard Assessment Tasks (SATs) results are made available to parents. Another problem might be that schools will have less flexibility about how they use their resources, if they are notionally tied to individualized identifications of needs. This may lead to less creativity in the use of resources. It may also divert attention away from looking at school solutions towards looking at individual problems. However, the evidence is that schools feel free to use their income as they see fit, no matter what the source of that income (Evans *et al.* 1994a).

A major disadvantage of the audit is said to be that it is very time-consuming, at least in the first year or so of its operation. However, the Code of Practice also requires identification and recording of special educational needs, so an Audit would seem to be a useful means of making use of data which have, in any case, to be collected by schools. The combination of the demands of the Code of Practice and the realization by LEAs that schools are more likely to be clear about the purpose of funding for SEN delegated via an audit may result in a widespread use of this mechanism to allocate SEN resources. The audit could also be extended to include levels of support for other additional needs, such as English for Speakers of Other Languages or giftedness. However, if the mechanism became too complicated, it might run foul of the prescription in Circular 2/94 that schemes must be 'as simple and clear as possible'.

How can accountability for the use of resources be ensured?

One of the key principles of LMS is that decisions about the use of delegated funds are best made at the school level. This being the case, all moneys coming into a school, no matter what their source, are allocated according to the priorities of the Head and Governors. The Audit Commission has published two documents about schools' management of their finances *Keeping Your Balance* (Ofsted/Audit Commission 1993) and *Adding up the Sums (*Audit Commission 1993), but neither of these addresses the question of the allocation of resources to various aspects of the schools' mission. No guidance is given to schools about this issue. There was some concern expressed in *Adding up the Sums* about schools holding large surplus balances, but most of the report was concerned about financial probity and not about the effectiveness of resource allocation in terms of educational priorities.

Allocating resources among competing educational priorities is therefore seen as a task for teachers and governors. There is evidence that some schools do not see special needs as a priority, and do not wish to attract pupils with special needs, and will therefore make minimal provision. Other schools, which make effective provision, tend to acquire a reputation for expertise in this area, and then attract more pupils with SEN, thus skewing their intake, which causes problems for them, particularly in the present competitive environment (Evans *et al.* 1994a).

LEAs have some difficulty in monitoring the use made of money delegated to schools specifically for SEN. They can call schools to account for the use of money delegated for pupils with statements, since the statement will give details of this, but it is difficult to monitor general SEN funds, particularly if the allocation mechanism is a general one, such as free school meals. If an audit is used, then LEAs will have a record of the identified needs within the school and the claims made for levels of resourcing. The Code of Practice also gives LEAs the opportunity to review a school's use of resources at the point that a child is referred for a statutory assessment.

Accountability for the use of SEN resources appears, therefore, to be relatively weak and ill-defined. Governors are ultimately accountable at school level. If governors are sympathetic and aware about special needs, then they can ensure that their school makes effective use of its resources. If they have other priorities, then it is difficult to see what mechanisms can be used to ensure that pupils with SEN have their needs met adequately.

Evaluation of cost-effectiveness

There have been few attempts to evaluate the cost-effectiveness of various forms of provision for SEN. The Audit Commission (1992a) concluded that pupils with moderate learning difficulties in primary school classrooms were receiving an education which was as effective as that delivered in a special school. In 1993 the Spastics Society and Coopers and Lybrand (NUT/Spastics Society 1993) costed various forms of provision for pupils with sensory and physical impairment but did not assess the relative effectiveness of these. The literature on integration makes assumptions about the relative benefits of integrated placements, but does not relate these to costs (Bennett and Cass 1989; Booth *et al.* 1992). Some LEAs (such as Northamptonshire and Leeds) have attempted to cost varying levels of support for SEN, but these have not yet been related to pupil outcomes.

This is an area where much more work needs to be done. Funding special education is an area fraught with problems of values and philosophies. However, the lack of clarity which presently exists about the effectiveness of different forms of provision makes it difficult for LEAs, schools and parents to make informed decisions.

Conclusions

Funding special educational provision is an area which highlights many of the issues and problems around the concept of special education. The 1981 and 1993 Acts defined special educational needs and provision in such a way that one depends upon the other. Special educational provision is 'provision which is additional to or otherwise different from' provision which is made generally within an area. Special educational needs are 'learning difficulties which call for special educational provision to be made' (DFE 1993). Thus, both concepts are a matter for local definition and local judgement.

Resourcing such provision in the days before LMS was a comparatively simple matter. LEAs would provide extra resources to schools in the form of support teaching and extra staffing for special educational needs. If such resources were not deemed to be adequate, then pupils would be referred for statutory assessment. There were problems with this system, as attested by the House of Commons Education Committee (HOC 1993) and the Audit Commission (1992a) among others. Nevertheless, within LEAs, there was some degree of consistency about funding and provision.

With the advent of LMS and GM schools, the situation has become more complicated. Schools are now notionally funded to provide for the special needs of their pupils, unless those pupils have statements. There are fears that central support services for SEN will have to be cut in many LEAs (Bangs 1993), and many services have been reorganized so that they now have to be bought in by schools from their delegated budgets. A recent ESRC-funded study (Evans *et al.* 1994a, 1994b) has indicated that these changes in funding arrangements have led to an increase in demand for statements and less willingness on the part of schools to make provision for pupils with SEN from within their own resources. Schools are unclear about the extent of their responsibilities because the funding mechanisms themselves are unclear. Most schools in the ESRC study were unaware of how much they received for SEN provision, as it was not separately itemized in their budgets or earmarked specifically for SEN purposes. In some ways this is a positive move, in that SEN funding was used in some schools to create more flexibility in teaching arrangements (such as, smaller classes or team-teaching) but there appeared to be less willingness in schools to provide for the more problematic pupils, and thus a pressure from schools for statutory assessment of a growing number of children (Evans *et al.* 1994a, 1994b).

The main issues around funding, therefore, appear to be:

- lack of clarity about definitions of special educational needs and provision;
- lack of clarity about what LEAs and schools are responsible for providing;
- diffuse responsibilities for funding between LEAs and the FAS;
- the increasing use of statements to make individualized funding allocations.

9 / Major Themes Revisited

In previous chapters it has been argued that, although the framework for special education may have changed, the essential and unresolved issues have not. They now have to be reconsidered in relation to an educational market in which individual semi-independent institutions compete for attractive and rewarding students. This indicates a need for a further analysis of a number of aspects of special education. These include:

- the nature of needs;
- the origins of educational needs;
- the concept of a range of provision in a system based on semi-independent educational units;
- the concept of integration in a fragmented education system;
- the nature of special educational provision;
- the governance of education and accountability for special education;
- equity of provision from area to area;
- monitoring of quality standards in provision.

The nature of needs

The nature of needs has been discussed in some detail in Chapter 4. It may be helpful to restate the legal grounds for deciding that a child has a special educational need. They are that:

a child has a learning difficulty if:

(a) he has significantly greater difficulty in learning than the majority of children of his age
(b) he has a disability which either prevents or hinders him from making use of educational facilities of a kind generally provided for children of the same age in the schools within the area of the local authority
(c) he is under the age of five years and is, or would be if special educational provision were not made for him, likely to fall within paragraph (a) or (b) when over that age.

(Education Act 1993 Section 156)

Significant learning difficulties

The phrase 'significantly greater' raises two questions: (1) how an individual school can judge a learning difficulty to be greater than the majority of an age group and (2) how significance can be judged in the absence of agreed criteria? When the majority of schools in an area were maintained and managed by LEAs, it was possible for them to establish criteria for the existence of special educational needs.

The introduction of a National Curriculum and a national system of testing individual progress was not linked to special education procedures in any way. The DFE saw test results as a means of assessing school performance and creating league tables from which parents could make their choice based on success. No attempt has yet been made to use performance criteria based on the National Curriculum and testing as a basis for the establishment of special educational needs. Delegated management to primary and secondary schools has made governors responsible for administration and for the delivery of the National Curriculum and schools have to decide, independently, who has a special educational need. Although many parents and organizations are seeking national criteria for determining special educational needs, that is, significant learning difficulties, all the administrative changes introduced in the system focus on individuals and individual schools. Unless national attainment testing is used to provide some criteria for the existence of special educational needs, it is difficult to see how administrators can be assured that judgements about the degree and significance of a learning difficulty are consistent.

Disabilities

Although not themselves special educational needs, the establishment of a disability is an acceptable way to register a possible special educational need. In the first instance, obvious physical and sensory disabilities can be readily accepted as preventing or hindering learning. Similarly many of the conditions giving rise to marked intellectual disabilities are clearly defined. The disability basis for special educational needs is constantly being extended. Autism, speech and language disorders, fragile X syndrome, dyslexia and many others are being added to the list of disabilities which may give rise to learning difficulties. There are two problems with this approach. First, the existence of a special educational need is seen as due solely to an individual deficit when it may also be due to the inappropriateness of a curriculum and deficiencies in its presentation. Secondly, it does not take account of learning difficulties arising from the interaction of the individual with his or her environment and with others or from general psychological, social and educational circumstances.

The origins of needs

Most special educational needs have both an individual deficit (disability) and an interactive (context) origin. While the individual disability may give rise to needs, it is the contexts in which a person lives and learns which determine the nature and extent of needs (Skrtic 1991). But for parents and many others, the issue is that a child has a problem and therefore a diagnosis or label is sought and, as with analogous medical conditions, it is assumed that there must be a treatment.

In the case of special *educational* needs, it is the *educational context* which determines learning difficulties and this concept causes problems for those who have to work with it. It is much easier for administrators to define needs as individual deficits. It is difficult for them to take into account interactive factors. Even when relationships give rise to needs for example, in emotional difficulties, there is an attempt to distinguish between problems with an 'internal' causation (emotional and behaviour difficulties) and 'external' causation (disruptive and disrupting behaviour). DFE guidance suggests that the former fall within special education definitions and regulations and the latter do not.

Current administrative procedures can only deal with individuals. The Code is based on an individual deficit approach to special educational needs. Little or no account is taken of education as an interactive learning process between pupils and teachers. There is no specific provision in the system for dealing with special educational needs arising from inappropriate educational programmes and methods. The general inspection of schools, to be carried out every four years, is a very blunt instrument for dealing with this problem.

A range of provision

The Code of Practice for special education makes it plain that a range of provision is necessary to meet a range of needs. However, the new legislative framework has replaced an education system in which LEAs developed and administered special education policies for all schools in an area, with an educational market in which individual schools are each responsible for their own special education policies. While the Code lays down the procedures all schools must observe (at least in spirit), there are no criteria for the nature of provision schools are expected to make. It may now be difficult for LEAs to obtain reliable and comparable information about the provision made by primary and secondary schools in their areas.

Information is limited about what constitutes a reasonable range of provision accessible to a day pupil. The range of needs which can be met effectively in day special schools of different kinds is also far from clear. The introduction of grant-maintained special schools and the increased management freedom of LEA-maintained special schools has not made planning a range of provision any easier. LEAs are now expected to be purchasers of facilities and services for children who are the subject of statements. Their ability to plan a range of provision in their areas is severely limited and they may only be able to fill a few gaps in a range. Much more work is necessary to determine what should be the desirable and practical range of facilities and services in an area from which parents should be able to choose, and what should be the means of ensuring that such a range is available. There are also other more fundamental problems to be addressed. These include: defining the limits of provision; priorities in the use of finite resources; the time requirements of new procedures; and resource implications of different forms of provision.

Integration

During the 1960s and 1970s, there were strong social and educational pressures to give children, young people and adults with disabilities access to all the institutions and opportunities available to their contemporaries. Normalization and integration were concepts compatible with comprehensive education and the policies of the governments of the time for greater social equality for individuals (Welton and Evans 1986). Both the Warnock Report (DES 1978) and the 1981 Act accepted a general trend to educate more children with special educational needs in primary and secondary schools, although the Act made it clear that such moves should not be expensive or to the detriment of the education of other pupils. At the time, integration was seen in terms of location (being in the same school), social interaction (sharing social facilities and activities), and functional interaction (sharing the same educational programmes) (Hegarty *et al.* 1981; Hegarty 1987).

In practice, LEA policies varied and parent opinion was divided. A significant group of parents campaigned for more opportunities in regular schools while at the same time, another group, wanting the continued protection of the separate special school, campaigned for the retention of separate provision.

Until the 1988 Education Reform Act, integration was seen as a parental right of access for the children to a common primary and secondary school system managed by an LEA. The implementation of that Act changed the position of parents of children with special educational needs. Instead of gaining access to a single type of maintained school they had to seek access to a range of schools and colleges with varying attitudes to integration, and admission policies determined by governors.

Social and political attitudes had changed. Integration as an aspect of social cohesion lost general support. A more competitive approach was expected in schools with a degree of selection based on attainments. The fragmentation of the management of the school and college system, the introduction of city technology colleges and grant-maintained schools, and the local management of all schools meant it was no longer possible to develop and maintain an overall LEA integration policy. Parental choice in an educational market became the objective.

Integration within the education system has changed from being part of a general social movement to being an aspect of parental choice. The Parent's Charter (DFE 1994a) and a separate guide for parents of children with special educational needs (DFE 1994b) provide evidence of the increasingly important role of parental involvement. However, parental choice is increasingly dependent on school choice and school admission policies. Integration is not simply a means of ensuring that parents of children with special educational needs have the same range of choices for their children as other parents. Many such parents also expect a choice between provision in a mainstream primary or secondary school and provision in separate special schools. The current educational policy rooted in economic competition and personal choice is not sympathetic to social integration and as a result, the integration of disabled children, young people and adults into schools and society receives less priority. A reappraisal of the concept of integration and an analysis of the economics of minority choices are now necessary. The Audit Commission/HMI (1992a) and NUT/Spastics Society (1993) have attempted to do this, but their analyses have been hampered by a lack of sufficient reliable evaluative data on the outcome for pupils of integrated and segregated provision.

The nature of provision

Since the Warnock Report, there have been a number of criticisms about the concept of a continuum of special educational needs and a continuum of provision (see, for example, Booth 1994). This is because the concept does not take into account essential discontinuities and differences between types of need and types of provision. However, there is no such objection to recognizing a range of needs of different types and degrees of severity which require a matching range of provision.

The 1993 legislation and Code of Practice raise a number of questions about the nature of provision. Some have already been mentioned in Chapter 4. For example, when is an individual education programme a special education one? These additional questions are concerned with the nature of provision. They include:

- what are the limits of provision;
- what is it about the programme that makes it special education;
- what is the nature or quality of additional teaching or non-teaching time that makes it special educational provision?

It may be helpful to start this analysis with the individual programme devised at Stage 1 in the Code of Practice. For example, if a teacher with special education qualifications and experience helps to plan the programme, it could be said to be a special education programme. The programme could be delivered by the regular class teacher with or without additional teaching or non-teaching help. The programme may or may not be regularly supervised by a special education teacher. What are the necessary conditions for special education to be provided? Should they include the quality of the extra time (the training and experience of the teacher or assistant)? Should a condition be that there is regular supervision by a special education teacher? Is it the supervision of the additional time or the skills of the person using it with pupils that constitutes special education? Is the programme, its delivery or its supervision special educational provision? Operational decisions will be necessary. Do those concerned with the field of special education have views? It would be a pity if it was left to the new Tribunals to decide.

It would seem sensible to define arrangements as *special* education when a trained and experienced special education teacher is responsible for the programme, its supervision and its outcome, whoever administers it. If this approach is accepted, then the Code makes it essential for every school, or cluster of schools, to have a trained special education teacher on the staff or to employ an appropriately qualified member of a support-teaching service on a regular basis.

Other forms of provision, such as units in primary and secondary schools and special schools, are easier to define. Staff qualifications, facilities and curriculum delivery can be specified for different kinds of special educational needs.

Governance and accountability

Prior to the 1988 and 1993 legislation (ERA 1988, EA 1993), responsibilities for special education were clear. Overall responsibility for provision rested with LEAs. They could plan and administer a range of services and facilities, including units in regular schools, special schools and advisory and support services. Other provision in non-maintained special schools and independent schools was approved by the DES/DFE. HM Inspectorate inspected both schools and units and LEA provision as a whole. Inspectorate reports supplied the information to enable the DES/DFE to carry out its legal responsibilities for special education.

LEAs continue to have overall responsibility for securing special education, but are expected to be purchasers of provision. Although they can influence policies in LEA-maintained schools, their responsibility for provision in both LEA-maintained and grant-maintained primary and secondary schools is limited to arrangements for pupils who are the subject of statements. Similarly, they have more limited powers with respect to the provision made by LEA-maintained and grant-maintained special schools. The FAS is responsible for elements in grant-maintained school budgets to cover special educational provision and also has powers to set up and finance grant-maintained special schools.

The governance of education is now divided between the FAS, LEAs and individual school governing bodies. Although the accountability of the three elements is clearly defined, responsibilities for planned and coordinated action by the FAS and an LEA and between an LEA and schools in an area, are less certain. Accountability for special educational provision, as outlined in the previous paragraph, is a case in point.

Equity

Parents of children with special educational needs expect a similar range and standard of provision wherever they live. The evidence produced by parents and voluntary organizations for the House of Commons Education Committee in 1992 underlined this view. The DFE was expected to establish national criteria for statements of needs and for provision to meet them (HOC 1993).

The response of the DFE to these wishes was *A Code of Practice for the Identification and Assessment of Special Educational Needs* (DFE 1994g). As the title implies, the implementation of the Code will ensure that LEA procedures for assessment and decision-making are similar and that there are agreed standards for the process of making statements. However, criteria for provision are very general, and there is no requirement that a particular range of provision should be available. Elaborate procedures for deciding the nature of a child's needs are set out, but the ways in which these needs should be met are not defined. This may be part of a policy to limit expenditure. If you do not define provision you do not sanction or require the use of resources. One consequence of this approach is that equity for parents is more likely to be determined by the decisions of special education Tribunals.

Monitoring

The monitoring of the education system as a whole will be by national attainment tests administered three times during a pupil's school life and by regular inspections by teams supervised by Ofsted. Parental choice of school is also intended to act as another means of monitoring school effectiveness. The question to be answered is whether these means will be appropriate for monitoring special educational provision and evaluating its effectiveness. The Minister told the Select Committee in 1993:

> . . . It is a combination, is it not, of the parents to start with? The front line of monitoring in a very real sense, is the parents themselves . . . Then there is a further measure, which is the Governors of the school have a responsibility in statute and the Code for ensuring the school policy on special educational needs . . . how far that policy is being fulfilled. Ofsted will have a role in its periodic inspections, in satisfying itself that the school is performing to its published policy and that pupils who have been identified within the framework of the Code's procedures as having special educational needs, are indeed having them properly catered for . . .
>
> (HOC 1993: Minutes of Evidence 9.2.94, para. 25)

Inspection procedures specify attention to special educational arrangements, but the programme supervised by Ofsted will be confined to individual schools. There is little evidence that there will be inspections of the range of facilities and services in an area. A second check on special education in schools is the annual report to parents. Experience to date suggests that attendance at meetings to receive reports is sparse and that active parents tend to have other interests (HOC 1993: xix).

Although HM Inspectorate has experience in the evaluation of special education, much of the evidence it receives will be second-hand through the reports of registered inspectors. General standards will be known, but the detailed evaluation of different ways of meeting needs will not. The higher education sector could make an important contribution to evaluation, but few special education departments have yet published significant data on these issues.

Teacher training

There have been government grants for special education teacher training in recent years, mainly for special educational needs coordinators in primary and secondary schools. Many teachers in the field have acquired additional qualifications, either diplomas or higher degrees. However, there is no requirement for teachers providing special education to have additional training or a specialist qualification.

New patterns of initial teacher training are being introduced for graduates. More graduate training is to be done in schools approved for the purpose. The BEd degree course is being shortened from four to three years. Both these changes will make it difficult to find time for an adequate special needs element in initial training.

The training implications of the EA 1993 and the Code are considerable. Not only do governors require training about their new responsibilities for special educational needs, but each school will also need to have available teachers with the necessary expertise. It will be necessary to identify the skills and experience required by primary and secondary schools to carry out their duties and to provide training opportunities.

Statements to define special educational needs

The EA 1993 and the Code of Practice make primary and secondary schools responsible for special educational needs which are not the subject of statements. Responsibilities and procedures are specified in some detail in the Code. Governors and senior management are also expected to make provision for a range of other special needs, such as disruptive behaviour (see Chapter 4).

Singling out special *educational* needs as the subject of a Code of Practice could unbalance a school's approach to the wider range of needs in its population. It could be argued that meeting *all* special needs, including special educational needs, should be a school's response to the different backgrounds, rates and styles of learning of the pupils it accepts.

Since the 1981 Act, the DES/DFE has given greater attention to meeting the needs of pupils with statements than to provision for a wide range of needs within the pupil population. The Audit Commission has published guidelines for the more effective use of the statutory assessment procedures (Audit Commission 1992a). The EA 1993 separates non-statement provision from statement provision, for which LEAs are responsible. Because most of the less severe learning and behaviour difficulties in primary and secondary schools arise from circumstances and contexts, rather than marked individual deficits, one option (discussed in the next chapter) may be to limit the scope of *special* education to pupils who are the subject of statements. This may encourage resources available in schools to meet the wide range of special needs, to be devoted to whole-school approaches and not concentrated on individuals.

Inter-agency cooperation

Inter-agency cooperation should be a feature of all assessment procedures and provision to meet special educational needs and the Code makes plain its importance. In practice, it is most likely to be developed as an integral part of statutory assessment procedures. But exhortations to work together have not resolved fundamental problems relating to the different priorities of health, social service and education authorities. Legislation has not helped. Education, Health and Social Services Acts all define disability and needs differently. The *Disabled Persons Act 1986*, which provides for continuity of support after school, uses employment definitions of disability coined some 40 years earlier. The *Children Act 1989*, which requires social service departments to keep a register of children with special needs, uses different definitions from the 1981 and 1993 Education Acts.

Each government and local authority department is, in practice, defining its own client population and developing its own priorities. From such a position, joint planning and joint provision for individuals are hard to achieve.

Parents

Parental choice of school has been at the heart of government education policy. For many parents, this is the most important decision they can make about their children's future. Schools now have to provide more information to facilitate choice. As schools now determine their own admission policies and are increasingly allowed to specialize, a school's choice may be more significant than a parent's. Choice for parents whose children have special educational needs has hitherto been more limited. This is due to the weight given to professional assessments and the slow development of professional partnerships with parents. In some instances, it has also been due to parents' perceived involvement in their children's problems, as in the case of behaviour difficulties. Recent legislation has given parents of children with special educational needs more freedom of choice, particularly if their children are the subject of statements. Perhaps of greater importance is the right of dissatisfied parents to go to an independent tribunal, rather than to one set up by the LEA.

Tribunals

Sections 177 to 181 of the EA 1993 establish the Special Educational Needs Tribunal to replace both local appeal procedures and appeals to the Secretary of State. However, the introduction of the Code of Practice is intended to create better relationships between parents, LEAs and schools and limit the need for a Tribunal. The Tribunal started work on 1 September 1994. The Lord Chancellor appointed a President, Trevor Aldridge, and a number of other legally qualified people to act as chairpersons. The Secretary of State for Education appointed a panel of 80 lay members, two of whom will sit with a chairperson at each hearing. The Tribunal will consider appeals against decisions made on or after 1 September 1994 and its decisions will be binding on LEAs. It will exercise its functions independently of central and local government, and members will be appointed to sit in Wales or in one of eight regions in England.

Regulations set out the procedures to be followed. Parents can make an appeal to the Tribunal on six grounds on which are:

- if an LEA refuses a parental request for an assessment;
- if an LEA refuses to make a statement for a child;
- if an parent is dissatisfied with the nature of LEA's statement;
- if an LEA refuses to reassess a child who has a statement;
- if an LEA decides to cease to maintain a statement;
- if an LEA refuses to change the name of the school specified in Part IV of the statement.

The aim is to make procedures as informal as possible and to discourage legal representation while at the same time encouraging parents to bring a *befriender* with them. This will be a person chosen by the parents to be with them at the Tribunal. LEAs are encouraged to prepare lists of people prepared to be befrienders and to make these available to parents. Voluntary organizations are likely to be a prime source of people willing and competent to act in this role. While it could be expected that articulate parents will make use of the Tribunal, it is claimed that every effort will be made to make less confident parents feel at ease.

At the time the Tribunal was set up, there was no idea of the number of appeals that might be expected. On the one hand, there were those who thought that the Code would improve procedures and lead to less disagreement about needs and provision. On the other, there were many who considered that more parents would appeal to an independent body than appealed to LEAs. At the time of writing, it is not possible to gauge the extent to which appeals will be made or the influence of Tribunal decisions on LEA practices. If the evidence of industrial tribunals is relevant to special education, tribunal decisions will have the potential seriously to distort LEA budgets.

Conclusion

This review of major themes shows that in spite of the positive advances made by new legislation, fundamental problems in special education remain. Although the definitions of needs and responsibilities for meeting them are laid down in the Code of Practice, responsibilities for provision are fragmented. There is no clarification of what does and what does not constitute provision nor of the minimum range of choice to which parents of children with special educational needs are entitled. It is argued here that the scope of provision should be reconsidered. The final chapter is concerned with an agenda for the future for the different contributors to the field.

10 / An Agenda for the Future

Although the new legislative framework is an improvement, an opportunity has been lost to reconcile the aims of primary and secondary education with a previously well-established approach to special education. The delegation of increased responsibilities and the introduction of a constantly changing National Curriculum and examination system continue to preoccupy schools and colleges. The search for higher standards has resulted in little attention being paid to a rationale for meeting the needs of pupils and students who are harder to teach, particularly those with identified special needs and special educational needs.

The lack of reconciliation between policies for education in general and special education in particular is not a weakness just in DFE policy development. Other interested parties, including higher education, have not apparently been very active in developing a new rationale for special education. While major changes in the education system have been taking place, most special education professionals and voluntary organizations have continued to believe in an open-ended commitment to meeting all special educational needs. Professionals and advocates have been responding to demands in a case-specific, *ad hoc* way and have failed to recognize resource limitations or the need for priorities. However, a number of LEA administrators have been attempting to develop a rational approach to resource allocation and management, as the examples in Chapter 6 illustrate.

The Code of Practice has endorsed and perpetuated existing stages of assessment and placed the individual education programme at the centre of provision. Little account seems to have been taken of realities in schools, where a lack of time and expertise may inhibit the development of well-informed special education policies. These drawbacks can be overcome in time and should not obscure the many positive benefits for schools and colleges of delegated management. In the meantime, it is important to ensure that special education becomes an integral part of management practices.

The DFE has made clear how the new legislation is to be implemented. However, reliance on the development of a market has made it difficult to detect a sense of direction and purpose for special education. It is time to give serious consideration to the implications of market-led educational policies for the effective management of special educational provision.

Principles and values

Special education has had its own value system which, in earlier times, was compatible with the values of an inclusive comprehensive education system. Recent changes in the education system have been informed by different principles, both implicit and explicit. The allocation of resources is being governed by outcomes. Little weight appears to be given to the quality of the education through which outcomes are achieved or of the value added by education to personal development and competence (Cordingley and Kogan 1993). Special education is now being influenced by a new set of values – competition, choice and selection on merit – which inform policies for schools and colleges.

The economic consequences of educational policies are now more clearly defined. High standards are necessary for successful international businesses and industries. They are seeking better educated and trained staff to become part of a 'world class' work-force. Whether higher standards for all are achieved by elitism and selection, at the expense of the harder to educate, is not always considered. What is certain is that the values of a market support success and penalize failure. It is important to ask whose failure? It may be acceptable for ineffective schools and colleges to go out of business, but institutional failure affects the prospects of pupils and students. What can the educational market do to support and to compensate the victims of its failures? Short-term solutions, which may separate apparent educational failures in different or special schools, are not good enough. On leaving school, everyone will be living in the same society and either contributing to it or being a drain on resources. It is short-sighted to consider only the value of the most able and those with the highest achievements (Housden 1993). The long-term costs of an inadequate and inappropriate education for less successful learners will soon deplete the resources that high achievers generate.

These are some of the issues which arise when considering provision for pupils and students with disabilities and learning difficulties. Because educational values reflect society's attitudes, there is a need to reconcile the different values which informed the 1981 and 1993 Education Acts and agree goals for education for all. There is every justification for seeking greater accountability in the field of special education, but an unmanaged market will not necessarily result in equity for those whose education requires more than average resources.

While supporting a competitive system, many parents want good education for less academic children. They also display generous and charitable attitudes to the educational needs of children who are disabled, as long as they do not interfere with their children's education. But parents are not the only contributors to a value system.

Changing relationships in the system

Apart from their continued responsibility for special educational provision for pupils who are the subject of statements, government policy has reduced the powers of LEAs by introducing local management and encouraging schools to seek grant-maintained status. At the time of writing, the impetus to seek grant-maintained status has decreased unless the existence of a school is threatened. By late 1994, only about 1 in 25 had given up LEA-maintained status and the proportion of negative parental ballots was increasing.

It is the changed relationship in the LEA-maintained sector which will be significant for special education. At present, there is a dependency culture in which schools continue to rely on LEAs for support. Some LEAs continue to act as if they determined school policies. While they still have powers to allocate resources within LMS, they have no control over their use within schools. LEAs will increasingly be expected to provide the services which schools demand (and, in some cases, are prepared to pay for), and not what the LEA thinks they need. It will take some time before schools recognize that they are the unit of account. Colleges of further education have responded to their independence and are working to satisfy markets which pay.

LEAs, as the main purchasers of special educational provision, will face two new difficulties. They will have very limited powers to create new facilities and services and they will have to finance the reasonable choices of provision made by parents. They will have to pay for psychological, education welfare services and support-teaching services for pupils who are the subject of statutory assessment and who have statements, but they will be expected to purchase most of the provision required from semi-independent contractors. While they are also expected to have policies for special educational provision, these will be purchasing policies which, however, may be distorted by Tribunal decisions about individual cases. In shifting responsibilities from LEAs to schools and colleges, the DFE has made it much more difficult to develop a managed system of special educational provision.

Questions

It is not possible to develop even a limited special education policy without considering societal and educational value systems. We need to be clear about the implications of education policies for all, including those with special educational needs. Administrators and professionals have to find the answer to a number of practical questions. Many are raised by Evans and Lunt (1994). Others arise from discussion in previous chapters. Some of these questions are:

Policy questions

DFE policy

- Has the DFE a special education policy?
- How do current policies to raise educational standards address the needs of pupils and students who are harder to teach?
- Will the creation of an internal market of independent providers result in an adequate and equitable range of special educational provision nationally?

LEA policies

- Will LEAs as purchasers be able to develop effective special educational policies for provision?
- With fragmented responsibilities for provision, how can LEAs ensure that there is an equitable range of provision in their areas?
- How will LEA and FAS policies for provision be coordinated to develop a coherent range of provision in an area?
- What will be the effect of a greater number of small unitary local authorities on policies and provision?

School and college policies

- How will the compatibility and appropriateness of school and college policies for pupils and students with disabilities and learning difficulties be assured in an LEA area?
- How will the influence of funding agencies (DFE, FEFC, FAS) on school and college policies be monitored?
- How will the training needs of schools and college policies be evaluated, financed and met?

Provision questions

Criteria

- What are the parameters of acceptable special educational provision?
- How is provision to be defined and safeguarded for pupils who are not the subject of statements?
- Will the Ofsted programme of relatively infrequent inspections result in acceptable criteria for the appropriateness and quality of provision?

Responsibilities

- Who is responsible for ensuring that an adequate range of provision is available in an area and for monitoring its quality?
- Who will ensure that governors and senior managers are well enough informed to implement the Code and develop school and college special needs policies?

Resources

- Will the equitable distribution of resources to schools and colleges for special needs be assured by a common funding formula?
- What should be the balance between resources allocated to schools to meet special needs and resources allocated for provision specified in statements?
- How can the effective use of resources delegated to schools be ensured?
- Are any steps necessary to ensure that Tribunal decisions do not distort the use of resources?

Parents

- What is the true extent of parental choice?
- How can parents be helped to exercise their right to choose provision?

Continuity

- How can an LEA ensure continuity in provision and services, from the early years to adulthood, for parents and their children in the education market?
- Given the fragmentation of educational responsibilities, how will the effective inter-agency cooperation required by the Code be developed and delivered?
- What steps can be taken to implement effective inter-agency transition plans for individuals who are disabled?

Other questions could be added, but these encapsulate the main management concerns.

Special educational principles

For all contributors to special education, answers to the questions above form one agenda with which this chapter is concerned. Many involved in special education continue to advocate needs-led provision at a time when education is being increasingly resource determined. Policies and programmes should be based on principles and special education interests must articulate principles for resource allocation and adopt priorities based on them. A number of principles inform the approach of the authors. They owe a great deal to the list prepared by Lunt and Evans (1994). These principles are that:

- the allocation of resources should be clear and easily understood and the accountability for their use should be unequivocal;
- the effective use of resources requires that there is a rational and coherent plan for an agreed range of special educational provision;
- the effective use of resources requires that there is an appropriate system of evaluating the cost and success of different forms of provision;
- allocation procedures should encourage the minimal identification of individual pupils and students as having special educational needs;
- allocation procedures for schools should embrace an agreed range of special educational provision in primary, secondary and special schools of all kinds, and elsewhere, for pupils with and without statements;
- all pupils with special educational needs, regardless of the nature of their needs, should have access to the same range of educational provision as children of the same age;
- allocation procedures post-school should ensure that all with recognized disabilities and learning difficulties should have access to an agreed range of further education and vocational training opportunities;

- allocation procedures should be equitable and based on determining levels of need and resourcing them accordingly;
- resources should be safeguarded for the very small minority of pupils and students with severe and complex special educational needs, who often require provision from the early years to adulthood;
- resources to meet those special educational needs not requiring a statement should be allocated to schools according to agreed criteria which reflect differences in demographic factors in their pupil intake;
- devolved management and finance requires that there is effective monitoring of delegated responsibilities and of the use of resources;
- the development of an agreed range of provision should be related to the degree and nature of parental choices.

These principles provide a basis for judging the appropriateness of special educational management and financing systems. Positive proposals for the future of special educational provision should take them into account.

Principles in action

While the Warnock Report's concept of a continuum of special educational needs was helpful in identifying the common ground between special and remedial education, it concealed important discontinuities. Without polarizing needs, some children require teachers with specialized knowledge, techniques, equipment and materials appropriate for their disabilities. Other children with special educational needs require good teaching, curriculum modification, and in some instances, appropriate environments. Although these two groups overlap, they mirror a rough division between LEA and school responsibilities and between methods of resource allocation. Individuals in both groups need to be identified, but whereas resources for the first group need to be allocated individually, perhaps in statements, resources for the second group should be included as an element for all special needs, in school-funding formulae.

The principles already outlined require that individually identified and resourced special educational needs should be kept to a minimum. Most of the complex sensory, physical and intellectual disabilities should be known before entry to school. Although some emerge later as a result of accidents, trauma, and other causes, the scale of future significant needs can be estimated. However, in many instances, the provision that individuals require can only be assessed by their response to education.

Minimizing identified individual special educational needs requires schools to be responsible for most special needs. Since the Warnock Report, the tendency has been to consider up to a fifth of the school population as having such needs at some time in their school career. Singling out special educational needs – defined by Stages 1 to 3 in the Code – from other special needs in schools, may have disadvantages. Concentration on individual programmes may be to the detriment of the development of relevant education for the majority of less successful and harder to teach pupils. The label 'special educational needs' may be used as an alibi for inaction (Booth 1994; Fulcher 1989) and lead to disputes about school and LEA responsibilities.

Options

It is important to consider: how individual resourcing can be minimized; how to make more consistent provision for the small percentage of children with marked disabilities and learning difficulties; and how schools of all types and sizes can develop an agreed range of provision for all the special needs in the populations for which they are responsible.

There are a limited number of policy options and three suggest themselves:

1 a status quo concentrating on the implementation of the Education Act 1993 and the Code of Practice;
2 an extension of the principles of the Code to all special needs in schools;
3 the restriction of the term special educational needs to individuals identified by statutory assessment procedures and who are the subject of statements.

Option 1

The advantage of this option is that there is a clear focus on special educational needs as legally defined. Disadvantages include the increased identification of individuals, the possible diversion of attention from other special needs and less attention to those aspects of the school programme which may create needs. The implementation of the current legislation will take time and require new LEA and school special education policies which recognize the changed power structure. Resources will have to be devoted to ensuring that all schools have special educational expertise readily available. Training for governors, senior managers and SEN coordinators will be necessary.

Option 2

The second option would require schools to look at all the special needs in their populations. It would entail a whole-school approach to the variety of needs with which most schools have to deal (see Chapter 4). The procedures of the Code – Stages 1 to 3 – would be initiated for all individuals whose needs could not reasonably be met by schools. At this point LEAs would be expected to respond accordingly.

The advantages of this option might be that:

- available resources would be devoted to school organization and curriculum delivery;
- additional finance to meet a variety of special needs would not necessarily be related to identified individuals;
- schools would be less inclined to label individuals.

However, disadvantages might include less knowledge and understanding of particular special needs and less specialist provision in primary and secondary schools.

Option 3

The third option would build on Option 2 and imply that only very significant special educational needs should be registered. Confining provision to that made for pupils with statements would have a number of advantages:

- the resourcing of individual children would be limited;
- all children considered to have significant special educational needs would be comprehensively assessed by standard procedures;
- needs would be defined clearly and consistently within LEA areas;
- available provision would be more clearly defined by LEAs;
- provision for individuals would be specified in agreed statements;
- all special educational provision would be financed by LEAs.

There might be a number of negative effects of such a policy, such as decreased attention to learning problems of all kinds, an increasing number of children being put forward for statutory assessment, and formal assessment and statements being seen as a form of certification.

We suggest that in future, policies should work towards a combination of Options 2 and 3. Most needs should be seen in terms of interactions between pupils and teachers, pupils and other pupils, and pupils and the curriculum, and not simply as individual deficits. Schools should be expected to develop a flexible learning support policy to meet all special needs. They should be encouraged to be inclusive and flexible in their response to individual pupils and devote adequate resources to meeting special needs of all kinds. At the same time, they should be helped to define realistic limits for the provision they can make.

Effective psychological and support-teaching services are necessary to enable schools to make adequate provision and to support those responsible for it. This support, if effective, may be expected to limit the number of pupils referred to LEAs for other actions, including statutory assessment. Such services would also help LEAs to identify significant needs and to develop criteria for intervention. The implementation of Option 2 could be linked with Option 3. While there is no doubt that the registration of significant needs is essential, it is equally important to keep registration to a minimum. When significant needs emerge, the procedures outlined in the first three stages of the Code of Practice should be instituted. They are equally applicable to all special needs.

It is suggested that special educational needs should be determined by statutory assessment and the preparation of a statement. Provision would be determined by the LEA in two ways – by the facilities and services necessary to meet the objectives of statements and by the facilities and services that the LEA is prepared to purchase to enable parents to have a reasonable choice.

It is argued that a combination of Options 2 and 3 would enable schools to make a coherent response to a range of special needs. Current funding based on free school meals for example, is more closely related to the existence of special needs than special educational needs. If funding formulae based on an audit of all needs are introduced, it will be possible for schools to develop a planned system of learning support. It will enable LEA interventions of all kinds to be initiated by the same stages of school assessment.

Criteria for special educational provision

Whether or not the proposals in the previous sections are acceptable, the fragmented responsibilities for special education as now defined require agreed criteria for provision. If criteria for provision are to be established, they should not draw attention away from school responsibilities for all special needs. Those who are harder to teach should receive good quality education and the responsibility of all teachers to understand and to meet special needs of all kinds should not be diminished. Whatever changes might be introduced in future, criteria for special educational provision are essential. We recommend that, to provide special education of any kind and carry out the requirements of the Code, primary and secondary schools should:

- have members of staff with recognized qualifications and/or experience relevant to the assessment of and provision for the learning and behaviour difficulties commonly found in primary and secondary schools;

- in the absence of such a recognized member of staff, the school should make satisfactory arrangements to ensure that necessary expertise is regularly available to identify needs and oversee provision;
- ensure that all individual special education programmes for pupils are carried out under the direct supervision of teachers with recognized special educational qualifications and experience;
- ensure that all non-teaching assistants supporting individual special education programmes have recognized training for the work.

Psychological and support-teaching services should:

- actively oversee the development and implementation of the programmes they recommend;
- have regular sessions with individuals and groups receiving special education;
- ensure that special education teachers in such services have training appropriate to the particular disabilities and difficulties of the pupils for whom they are responsible.

Similar criteria should be applied to provision in special schools and units. It is important that parents, pupils and students, administrators and non-specialist teachers should be clear when special educational provision is being made and the entitlement of a pupil or student when it is offered. Some additions to the Parent's Charter will be necessary to clarify entitlements to provision. Quality standards for provision must be established and criteria for provision would be a first step.

Agendas for action

Major contributors to special education are now reviewing their activities in the light of the new framework and power structure for special education. They will develop agendas for the implementation of the new legislation and the Code. The following sections set out the items that the authors consider should be included in these agendas.

Primary and secondary schools

The Code of Practice and Statutory Regulations set out what is now required in a school's special education policy. It should include information about provision, policies for identification, assessment and individual provision, staffing and partnerships with bodies outside the school. An effective policy also requires the specification of available resources and their use.

Special education qualifications and experience

A first item on a school's agenda must be to identify members of staff with special education expertise. Schools are expected to have an SEN coordinator whose administrative and specialist activities are specified in the Code. The Code does not require the SEN coordinator to have special education qualifications or experience.

A number of questions are raised by this separation of administrative and professional responsibilities. Schools must consider whether:

- a senior manager or a teacher with recognized qualifications and/or experience with such needs should be the SEN coordinator;
- there are members of staff with recognized qualifications and/or experience of work with pupils with the special educational needs most commonly found in primary and secondary schools;
- in the absence of a member of staff with recognized qualifications and/or experience, appropriate steps have been taken to ensure that special education expertise is regularly available.

There are a number of ways of making expertise available (Lunt *et al.* 1994b). Many of them involve governors and senior managers working together on agreed lines in clusters or federations. Small primary schools might join a cluster to share special education expertise. Clusters of primary and secondary schools might ensure continuity between phases of schooling.

Time

Much teacher planning, report writing and contact with parents takes place outside the hours when children are being taught. But it has to be recognized that school time has to be set aside for SEN coordinators and special education teachers to assess children, to work with teachers and children in the classroom and to evaluate programmes. Staffing costs are high and it will be difficult for many schools to make available the time required to carry out the duties set out in the Code.

Training

Both teacher and non-teaching assistant time is currently available in schools. Budget limitations will make non-teaching time a more attractive option. Many of the teachers and non-teaching assistants helping pupils with special educational needs have little or no special training for the work. There will be many training needs to be met from school budgets or schools will have to purchase skilled teaching and non-teaching time.

Psychological Services

Legislation requires LEAs to provide psychological services and their financing is a mandatory exception to the delegation of funds to schools. Such services are expected to assist in statutory assessment and to support provision specified in statements. There has been general agreement that staffing should be on the basis of one psychologist to 8000 pupils. Where services work in the pre-school and post-school periods, additional staffing is necessary.

Educational psychologists have a tradition of working in schools to help teachers identify special needs of all kinds and make provision for them. Psychologists can contribute to the assessment and solution of many learning difficulties but few have had adequate training or experience with children with severe and complex sensory and physical disabilities. Although many work with individual children, few are in a position to provide special education themselves. However, a well-trained and managed educational psychology service is essential for the exercise of LEA special education responsibilities.

Psychological services must achieve a reasonable balance between time spent in assessment and advice and time spent working with teachers and pupils to meet needs. An agenda for services might include:

- helping teachers and schools to identify special needs;
- developing school audit methods to establish the extent of special needs of all kinds including special educational needs;
- helping schools to develop provision to meet the special needs for which they are responsible;
- contributing to statutory assessment procedures;
- contributing to the provision specified in statements;
- evaluating the effectiveness of provision;
- contributing to staff development programmes.

Education welfare services

Another mandatory service LEAs are expected to maintain is an education welfare service. Education Social Workers have long been the link between LEAs and families. In addition to their work with pupils and families about school attendance and other welfare matters, services have always made a significant contribution to special education.

Education social workers can help to prevent some special needs arising and to identify others. They can support parents and families during statutory assessment and when statements are made. They continue to play an important role in home-school liaison, when special educational provision is made by facilitating parental visits to schools and escorting their children to school. Education Welfare Services' links between primary and secondary schools and families are important in a number of other ways.

Some schools are now employing their own education social workers. These workers may be particularly helpful during family crises when pupils are exhibiting behaviour difficulties. Working with teachers, they can share their expertise about the nature and management of behaviour difficulties and ensure that parents and families are fully involved in helping to deal with them. An agenda for the Welfare Services should include:

- helping schools to understand the home circumstances of pupils;
- facilitating home-school links when special needs are identified;
- contributing to and helping parents to understand the statutory assessment procedures.

Support teaching services

In future, these services may be provided by LEAs or by independent contractors. LEAs are responsible for the supply or employment of the services necessary for statutory assessment and specified in statements. Schools may employ either LEA or independent services to support and to contribute to the provision for which they are responsible. The Code suggests that it would be helpful if schools and LEAs made service level agreements specifying the scope, quality and duration of services. It also states that:

> When schools enter contracts with private or voluntary sector providers they should satisfy themselves of the qualifications and experience of the specialists involved and that the service represents good value for money.
>
> (DFE 1994g: 2.59)

Agreed standards for support-teaching services are now essential and their approval should not be left to schools. It is not yet clear who will be responsible for protecting pupils and teachers and ensuring that services reach an adequate standard. Procedures to approve and license services should be put in place.

Size of services

The need for services is clear, but their size and nature are not. The House of Commons Committee could get no evidence on this point in 1993 (HOC 1993). There is very little evidence about the size of services for particular disabilities, or for areas, or pupil populations. An important item on the agenda of support-teaching services is the development of a database on the size, working patterns and effectiveness of the services.

Training

Services should employ trained and experienced special education teachers. Teachers offering support services to schools must be well trained and have sufficient experience to have credibility in schools. In addition to knowledge about disabilities, they require preparation to work cooperatively with others.

An agenda for these services, whether LEA or independent should include:

- making clear the kinds of special educational needs for which their staff have appropriate qualifications and experience;
- establishing their priorities and setting out the time requirements of their practices;
- setting out a service cost structure and a pricing system;
- describing the evaluation methods and performance criteria they employ.

Post-school provision

Although the FHEA 1992 gives both the FEFC and colleges responsibility for provision for students with disabilities and learning difficulties, there is no Code and no detailed specification of procedures. It is assumed that colleges will contribute to transition plans devised by LEAs and that the FEFC will finance provision with a recognized vocational objective. Much work is currently in progress to develop appropriate procedures for this group of students. The further education system has, in the past, been no more sympathetic than the school system to the problems of the harder to teach. The introduction of outcome-related funding is not making provision for this group, among whom are those with disabilities and learning difficulties, any easier.

The FEFC has set up a committee to consider their needs and its findings will set an agenda for colleges. Inducements have to be found to encourage colleges to meet all the educational needs in the communities they serve, and not just the simpler ones. While awaiting the recommendations of the Tomlinson Committee, colleges should be:

- clear about the importance of post-school provision for students with disabilities and learning difficulties;
- developing policies for learning support which facilitate the access of such students;

- involved in the transition reviews specified in the Code and carried out by LEAs;
- developing a range of provision for the students concerned;
- providing individual tutorial and other support to facilitate learning;
- concerned about the outcomes of their contribution to the individual needs of their students.

Local Education Authorities and the Funding Agency for Schools

The role of LEAs has been changed from a proactive one to a reactive one. Their responsibilities depend on referrals made by schools after having completed three stages of assessment. Although LEAs will be informed about primary and secondary arrangements, they may have little first-hand evidence about their appropriateness or effectiveness. They will be mainly required to secure and pay for the provision set out in statements. The work of the psychological and support-teaching services employed directly or on contract may be their only provision. LEAs will require policies for making statutory assessments and statements and for financing provision. Where new special school provision is required, FAS and LEA policies must be coordinated. The Code suggests that LEAs will need a moderating body to develop criteria for initiating assessments and making statements.

The new powers of parents to choose provision and to appeal to Tribunals make it essential for LEAs to develop policies which are clear and unequivocal. Parental appeals, voluntary organization pressures and Tribunal decisions can distort funding policies and the equitable distribution of resources. It is difficult to see how equity can be maintained in a competitive situation where it is now even likelier that the strongest and most articulate parents will be able to distort funding policies.

A particular problem for LEAs is the relationship between the costs of statement provision and the percentage of funds for special education allocated in school budgets. The agenda for LEAs is a complex one. They will have to:

- develop a special education policy to implement the Code of Practice;
- work with health authorities and social services to develop and implement procedures for meeting the special educational needs of children under five;
- collaborate with social services over the registration of needs during the school period;
- set up a moderating body to develop and monitor criteria for statutory assessment and making statements;
- set up procedures for multi-professional assessment with health and social services for determining needs and for specifying each agencies' contribution to provision;

- maintain sensitive contact with parents during assessment procedures and provide them with a clear choice of provision;
- secure the provision specified in statements and monitor its effectiveness;
- develop, in association with other agencies, a transition plan for individuals and ensure that appropriate post-school educational opportunities are available.

In addition LEAs, in collaboration with parents, will have to determine their approach to integration with particular reference to:

- how much provision they can afford to make for pupils with statements in primary and secondary schools;
- whether finance for pupils with statements will be retained or passed to the schools they attend;
- what choices of integrated or separate provision they can afford to offer to parents.

This is a formidable agenda and changes in local authority boundaries make it harder to deal with.

Social services departments

The agendas of LEAs cannot be considered in isolation from social services' responsibilities under the Children Act 1989, the Disabled Persons Act 1986 and the NHS and Community Care Act 1990. Social services departments are also responsible for much provision for children under five and for assessing post-school needs and securing provision for them.

Assessments and statements for children under five involve LEAs in close contact with other agencies. The Code says that LEAs should, wherever possible, use and build on a well-established network of relationships with social services departments, health authorities, NHS trusts, Family Health Service Authorities and the voluntary sector (DFE 1994g: 5.1). LEAs should also inform all those responsible for under-five provision, made under the aegis of social services, about their procedures for the identification of special educational needs.

The Code expects schools to make suitable arrangements for liaising with social services, for registering concerns about children's welfare, for putting into practice local child protection procedures, for liaising with the local authority about children looked after by the authority and for keeping informed about the services provided by the authority for children 'in need' (DFE 1994g: 2.57). Social services departments in their turn are expected to have designated officers for liaison with schools.

The Code states that the first annual review after a young person reaches the age of 14 should include a Transition Plan. LEAs must seek information from social services about whether a child has a disability under Sections 5 and 6 of the Disabled Persons Act 1986. Under the Children Act 1989 and the NHS and Community Care Act 1990 social services departments are required to arrange a multi-disciplinary assessment and provide care plans for children and adults with significant special needs, which may include the provision of further education (DFE 1994g: 6.50).

There remain many areas of uncertainty about definitions of need and responsibilities for post-school care and education. Resource limitations do not facilitate liaison or joint provision between agencies. In practice, many young people find it difficult to get the support they need in further and higher education.

Voluntary organizations

Before setting an agenda, it is important to put on record the significance of voluntary organizations which draw attention to and promote the interests of, individuals and their families. Many of the advances in provision have been initiated by them. However, it has to be recognized that there is a charity market with a pecking order which results in the less attractive needs having less influential advocates. The question is whether the campaigning energy of voluntary organizations can be harnessed within an equitable approach to meeting special educational needs. There is no doubt that organizations can work together as the Special Education Consortium (SEC) illustrated in its evidence to the House of Commons Education Committee (HOC 1993). What is less certain is their ability to coordinate their contributions to the development of an agreed range of provision for all needs.

Close contact between LEAs and voluntary organizations is expected in the Code of Practice. When statements are made, the LEA must give parents the name of a person who is available to give them advice and support. LEAs will look to voluntary organizations to provide suitable candidates for the role of named person. If parents decide to appeal to a Tribunal, they will be able to choose a befriender and again, voluntary organizations will be expected to provide such a person.

An agenda for voluntary organizations should include:

- continuing to identify the educational and related services necessary to meet specific needs;
- helping policy-makers to develop an appropriate range of special educational provision for under fives, in schools and in the post-school period;
- assisting parents to make informed choices of provision.

Central government

Although the DFE is responsible for the implementation of the Code, a number of other departments – Health, Housing, Employment and the Home Office – all make important contributions. The more complex the disabilities of children, young people and adults, the more necessary it is to develop a holistic approach to their needs. This requires well-developed inter-agency procedures for policy development and implementation. If collaboration is expected at local level, it must be evident at central government level.

The DFE should undertake a review of special education policy in the light of the conditions created by the EA 1993. Although the quality of individual institutional provision is to be monitored by inspection, there is no evidence of a similar approach to the monitoring of LEA policies, services to schools and the range of provision in an area. An agenda for the DFE should include:

- a commitment to integrate the education of pupils and students with disabilities and learning difficulties into educational policy making at the outset and not as a consequence of other decisions;
- a more precise definition of provision setting out criteria which specify when it is being made;
- giving consideration to confining the definition of special educational needs to children who are the subject of statements;
- the development of sensitive funding mechanisms to enable schools to respond to a wide range of special needs, including special educational needs, on a whole-school basis without identifying individuals;
- fostering the development of quality indicators for special education;
- exploring and implementing ways to reward schools for successful work with the harder to educate.

The DFE should also consider:

- how to ensure that an adequate range of facilities and services is available in each area or region;
- how standards of provision other than in schools are to be monitored;
- how to ensure that an equitable range of choice for parents of pupils with special educational needs is available nationally.

Final questions

In addition to the separate agendas outlined in this chapter, there are a number of general questions. Answers to them may be expected to emerge in the next few years. These questions include:

- Is equity for those with disabilities compatible with the creation of an educational market?
- What does integration mean in the educational market-place?
- Will the delegation of responsibilities to schools and colleges result in better provision for minorities with special needs?

Asking these questions helps to illuminate the new context for special education. The aim of these developments should be the minimum identification of individuals and the maximum emphasis on schools as responsible for the needs of most pupils arising from variations in their rates and styles of learning. A number of options for future development have been set out.

Answers to the questions can at present only be provisional, since it will be some time before the Acts are fully implemented and the effects of government funding policies are known. In the mean time, only aspirations are clear. The White Paper *Choice and Diversity* (DFE 1992a) set out the future aims of education for all. In the foreword, the Prime Minister says: 'I am not prepared to see children in some parts of this country having to settle for a second class education. Education can make or mar each child's prospects. Each has but one chance in life.'

The quality of that one chance is even more critical for children, young people and adults with disabilities and learning difficulties.

Bibliography

Adams, F.J. (ed.) (1990) *Special Education in the 1990s*. London: Longman.

Ainscow, M. (1991) Effective Schools for All: an alternative approach to special needs in education. *Cambridge Journal of Education*, 21(3): 293–308.

Ainscow, M. and Tweddle, D. (1979) *Preventing Classroom Failure*. Chichester: John Wiley and Sons.

Audit Commission (1993) *Adding up the Sums: Schools' Management of their Finances*. London: HMSO.

Audit Commission (1994) *The Act Moves On: Progress in Special Educational Needs*. London: HMSO.

Audit Commission/HMI (1992a) *Getting in on the Act. Provision for Pupils with Special Educational Needs: The National Picture*. London: HMSO.

Audit Commission/HMI (1992b) *Getting the Act Together. Provision for Pupils with Special Educational Needs: A Management Handbook*. London: HMSO.

Ball, S. (1990) *Politics and Policy Making in Education. Explorations in Policy Sociology*. London: Routledge.

Bangs, J. (1993) Support services: stability or erosion? *British Journal of Special Education*, 20(3): 105–7.

Barton, L. and Tomlinson, S. (eds) (1984) *Special Education and Social Interests*. Introduction. London: Croom Helm.

Bennett, N. and Cass, A. (1989) *From Special to Ordinary Schools. Case Studies in Integration*. London: Cassell.

Bibby, P. (1994) Dreamland of SEN draft, *Times Educational Supplement*, 18 February.

Booth, T. (1994) Continua or chimera? *British Journal of Special Education,* 21(1): 21–4.

Booth, T., Swann, W., Masterson, M. and Potts, P. (eds) (1992) *Policies for Diversity in Education.* London: Routledge.

Bowe, R. and Ball, S., with Gold, A. (1992) *Reforming Education and Changing Schools.* London: Routledge.

Cameron, R.J. (ed.) (1986) *Portage, Pre-schoolers and Professionals: Ten Years of Achievement in the UK.* Windsor: NFER-Nelson.

CCCS (1981) *Unpopular Education.* London: Hutchinson.

Cohen, R., Hughes, M., Ashworth, L. and Blair, M. (1994) *School's Out. The Family Perspective on School Exclusion.* London: Barnardo's and Family Service Units.

Collins, J.E. (1961) *The Effects of Remedial Education.* Birmingham: University of Birmingham Institute of Education.

Cordingley, P. and Kogan, M. (1993) *In Support of Education. Governing the Reformed System.* London: Jessica Kingsley Publishers.

Cowne, E. and Norwich, B. (1987) *Lessons in Partnership: An INSET Course.* Bedford Way Paper 31, London University Institute of Education.

DES (1963) *Half Our Future,* (The Newsom Report). London: HMSO.

DES (1967) *Children and their Primary Schools,* (The Plowden Report). London: HMSO.

DES (1970) *Education (Handicapped Children Act).* London: HMSO.

DES (1978) *Special Educational Needs. Report of the Committee of Enquiry into the Education of Handicapped Children and Young People,* (The Warnock Report). London: HMSO.

DES (1981) *Education Act.* London: HMSO.

DES (1988a) *Circular 7/88: The Local Management of Schools.* London: HMSO.

DES (1988b) *Education Reform Act.* London: HMSO.

DES (1989) *Assessments and Statements of Special Educational Needs: Procedures within the Education, Health and Social Services,* Circular 22/89. London: DES.

DES (1991) *Education and Training for the 21st Century,* White Paper. London: HMSO.

DFE (1992a) *Choice and Diversity,* White Paper. London: HMSO.

DFE (1992b) *Further and Higher Education Act.* London: HMSO.

DFE (1993) *Education Act 1993.* London: HMSO.

DFE (1994a) *Our Children's Education. The Updated Parent's Charter.* London: HMSO.

DFE (1994b) *Special Educational Needs: A Guide for Parents.* London: HMSO.

DFE (1994c) *The Development of Special Schools,* Circular 3/94. London: DFE.

DFE (1994d) *The Organisation of Special Educational Provision,* Circular 6/94. London: DFE.

DFE (1994e) *Pupils with Problems,* Circulars 8/94, 9/94, 10/94, 11/94, 12/94 and 13/94. London: DFE.

DFE (1994f) *Going Grant-maintained with other Schools: GM Clusters.* London: HMSO.

DFE (1994g) *A Code of Practice for the Identification and Assessment of Special Educational Needs.* London: HMSO.

DFE (1994h) *Local Management of Schools,* Circular 2/94. London: DFE.

DHSS (1970) *Chronic Sick and Disabled Act.* London: HMSO.

DHSS (1986) *Disabled Persons (Services, Consultation and Representation) Act.* London: HMSO.

DoH (1989) *The Children Act*. London: HMSO.

DoH (1990) *National Health Service and Community Care Act*. London: HMSO.

Evans, J., Everard, B., Friend, J., Glaser, A., Norwich, B., and Welton, J. (1989) *Decision-making for Special Needs: An Inter-service Resource Pack*. London: Institute of Education.

Evans, J. and Lunt, I. (1994) *Markets, Competition and Vulnerability: Some Effects of Recent Legislation on Pupils with Special Educational Needs*. London: Institute of Education and Tufnell Press (London File Series).

Evans, J., Lunt, I., Young, P. and Vincent, C. (1994a) Doing More with Less: Schools' Responses to SEN under LMS, paper given at *British Educational Research Association Conference*, Oxford, September.

Evans, J., Lunt, I., Young, P. and Vincent, C. (1994b) *Local Management of Schools and Special Educational Needs*. Final Report to the ESRC.

FEU (1989a) *Learning Support*. London: FEU.

FEU (1989b) *Towards a Framework for Curriculum Entitlement*. London: FEU.

FEU (1989c) *Working Together*. London: FEU.

FEU (1992) *Supporting Learning – A Model for Colleges*. London: FEU.

Fish, J. (1989) *What is Special Education?* Milton Keynes: Open University Press.

Ford, J., Mongon, D. and Whelan, M. (1982) *Special Education and Social Control: Invisible Disasters*. London: Routledge and Kegan Paul.

Fulcher, G. (1989) *Disabling Policies? A Comparative Approach to Education Policy and Disability*. London: Falmer Press.

Galton, M., Fogelman, K., Hargreaves, L. and Cavendish, S. (1991) *The Rural Schools Curriculum Enhancement National Evaluation (SCENE) Project*. Final Report. London: DES.

Goacher, B., Evans, J., Welton, J. and Wedell, K. (1988) *Policy and Provision for Special Educational Needs*. London: Cassell.

Gulliford, R. (1989) The development of special education: lessons from the past, in N. Jones (ed.) *Special Educational Needs Review. Vol. 1*. London: Falmer Press.

Hall, K. (1994) Conceptual and methodological flaws in the evaluation of the 'First' British Reading Recovery Programme, *British Educational Research Journal*, 20(1): 121–8.

Hegarty, S. (1987) *Meeting Special Needs in Ordinary Schools: An Overview*. London: Cassell.

Hegarty, S., Pocklington, K. and Lucas, D. (1981) *Educating Children with Special Educational Needs in the Ordinary Schools*. Slough: NFER.

Housden, P. (1993) *Bucking the Market: LEAs and Special Needs*. Stafford: NASEN.

House of Commons Education, Science and Arts Committee. (1987) *Third Report. Implementation of the Education Act 1981*. Vols I and II. London: HMSO.

House of Commons Education Committee. (1993) *Third Report. Meeting Special Educational Needs. Statements of Needs and Provision*. Vols I and II. London: HMSO.

ILEA (1985) *Educational Opportunities for All*, (The Fish Report). London: ILEA.

Jonathan, R. (1989) Choice and control in education: parental rights, individual liberties and social justice, *British Journal of Educational Studies*, 27(4): 321–38.

Jowett, S., Hegarty, S. and Moses, D. (1988) *Joining Forces. A Study of Links between Ordinary and Special Schools*. Windsor: NFER-Nelson.

Lee, T. (1992) Finding simple answers to complex questions: funding special needs under LMS, in G. Wallace (ed.) *Local Management of Schools. Research and Experience*. Clevedon: Multi-lingual Matters.

Levin, H. (1988) Cost-effectiveness and educational policy, *Educational Evaluation and Policy Analysis*, 10(1): 51–69.

Lunt, I. (1992) Recent judgements and their implications for educational psychologists, *DECP Newsletter No. 52*.

Lunt, I. and Evans, J. (1994) *Allocating Resources for Special Educational Needs Provision*. Stafford: NASEN.

Lunt, I., Evans, J., Norwich, B. and Wedell, K. (1994a) *Working Together: Inter-school Collaboration for Special Needs*. London: David Fulton.

Lunt, I., Evans, J., Norwich, B. and Wedell, K. (1994b) Collaborating to meet special educational needs: Effective clusters? *Support for Learning*, 9(2): 73–8.

McGinty, J. and Fish, J. (1992) *Learning Support for Young People in Transition*. Milton Keynes: Open University Press.

McGinty, J. and Fish, J. (1993) *Further Education in the Market Place*. London: Routledge.

Moses, D. and Hegarty, S. (1988) *Developing Expertise: INSET for Special Educational Needs*. Windsor: NFER-Nelson.

Moses, D., Hegarty, S. and Jowett, S. (1988) *Supporting Ordinary Schools: LEA Initiatives*. Windsor: NFER-Nelson.

National Commission on Education (1993) *Learning to Succeed*. London: Heinemann.

Norwich, B. (1990) *Reappraising Special Needs Education*. London: Cassell.

NUT/Spastics Society (1993) *Within Reach. The School Survey*. London: NUT.

OECD/CERI (1981) *The Education of the Handicapped Adolescent. Integration in the School*. Paris: OECD.

OECD/CERI (1985) *The Integration of the Handicapped in Secondary Schools. Five Case Studies*. Paris: OECD.

OECD/CERI (1986) *Young People with Handicaps – The Road to Adulthood*. Paris: OECD.

OECD/CERI (1988) *Disabled Youth – The Right to Adult Status*. Paris: OECD.

OECD/CERI (1991) *Disabled Youth – From School to Work*. Paris: OECD.

OECD/CERI (1994) *Disabled Youth and Employment*. Paris: OECD.

Ofsted/Audit Commission (1993) *Keeping Your Balance: Standards for Financial Administration in Schools*. London: Ofsted.

Portage Project (1976) *Portage Guide to Early Education*. Portage Wisconsin: Co-operative Service Agency.

Riddell, S., Brown, S. and Duffield, J. (1994) Conflicts of policies and models: the case of specific learning difficulties, in S. Riddell and S. Brown (eds) *Special Educational Needs Policy in the 1990s*. London: Routledge.

Robson, C., Sebba, J., Mittler, P. and Davies, G. (1988) *In-Service Training for Special Educational Needs: Running Short School-Focused Courses*. Manchester: Manchester University Press.

Russell, P. (1990) Implications for special educational needs, in M. Flude and M. Hammer (eds) *The Education Reform Act 1988: Its Origins and Implications*. London: Falmer Press.

Skrtic, T. (1991) Students with Special Educational Needs: Artifacts of the Traditional Curriculum, in Ainscow, M. (ed.) *Effective Schools for All*. London: David Fulton.

Stowell, R. (1987) *Catching Up? Provision for Students with Special Educational Needs in Further and Higher Education*. London: National Bureau for Handicapped Students.

Thomas, H. (1990) From local financial management to local management of schools, in M. Flude and M. Hammer (eds) *The Education Reform Act 1988: Its Origins and Implications*. London: Falmer Press.

Thomas, H. and Bullock, A. (1994) Money, monitoring and management, in P. Ribbins and E. Burridge (eds) *Improving Education: Promoting Quality in Schools*. London: Cassell.

Tomlinson, S. (1982) *A Sociology of Special Education*. London: Routledge and Kegan Paul.

Vincent, A.T. (1989) *New Technology, Disability and Special Educational Needs*. Coventry: Empathy Ltd. Hereward College.

Wade, B. and Moore, M. (1993) *Experiencing Special Education*. London: Cassell.

Warfield, M.E. (1994) A cost-effectiveness analysis of early intervention services in Massachusetts: implications for policy, *Educational Evaluation and Policy Analysis*, 16(1): 87–100.

Wedell, K. (1990) The 1988 Act and current principles of special educational needs, in H. Daniels and J. Ware (eds) *Special Educational Needs and the National Curriculum*. London: Institute of Education and Kogan Page.

Wedell, K. (1995) *Putting the Code of Practice into Practice*. London: Institute of Education.

Welton, J. and Evans, J. (1986) The development and implementation of special education policy: where did the 1981 Act fit in? *Public Administration*, 64: 209–27.

Wright, A. (1992) Evaluation of the first British Reading Recovery Programme, *British Educational Research Journal*, 18(4): 351–68.

Wright, A. (1994) Evaluation of Reading Recovery in Surrey. A reply to Kathleen Hall, *BERJ*, 20(1): 129.

INDEX